MW00903329

DORM ROOM
DEVOTIONS

COMPILED BY
JIM HAMPTON

Beacon Hill Press of Kansas City
Kansas City, Missouri

Copyright 2002
by Beacon Hill Press of Kansas City

ISBN 083-412-0232

Printed in the
United States of America

Cover Design: Ted Ferguson

Library of Congress Cataloging-in-Publication Data
Dorm room devotions / compiled by Jim Hampton
    p. cm.
  ISBN 0-8341-2023-2 (pbk.)
  1. College students—Religious life. I. Hampton, Jim, 1966-
    BV4531.3 .D67 2002
    242'.634—dc21

                                                    2002011461

10 9 8 7 6 5 4 3 2 1

This book is dedicated to the thousands of college and university students with whom we have had the privilege of journeying together. It is our hope that we have touched your lives as much as you have touched ours.

CONTENTS

Part 3: Ministry

Part 4: Life Skills

ABOUT THE AUTHORS

Tyler Blake is an English professor and department chairperson at MidAmerica Nazarene University in Olathe, Kansas. He considers himself to be "the baddest old-school rapper" in Nazarene higher education.

Dean Blevins is an associate professor of Christian education at Trevecca Nazarene University in Nashville. For fun, he enjoys bowling with his daughter, Rachel, and relaxing with a Louis L'Amour western novel.

Kim Follis is the dean of student development at Canadian Nazarene University College in Calgary.

Jim Hampton serves as youth product editor for Barefoot Ministries of Nazarene Publishing House in Kansas City. He spends his free time collecting baseball memorabilia from the 1975 and 1976 World Series champion Cincinnati Reds, arguably the greatest team ever.

Elliot Johnson is the head baseball coach and professor of exercise and sports science at Olivet Nazarene University in Bourbonnais, Illinois. For recreation he likes to run four miles through the state park located near the university.

Jan Simonson Lanham is a professor of psychology at Eastern Nazarene College in Wollaston, Massachusetts. To unwind, she likes nothing better than to sit by the ocean with her camera and take pictures.

Diane LeClerc serves as professor of theology and church history at Northwest Nazarene University in Nampa, Idaho. A little-known fact about Diane is that she was the first girl to play on the Little League baseball team in her hometown.

Gary Sivewright is chaplain and vice president of campus ministries at Mount Vernon Nazarene University in Mount Vernon, Ohio. Gary's idea of heaven (this side of earth) is watching the Kansas City Royals or the Kansas City Chiefs with a plate of nachos on his lap and a Diet Coke in his hand.

Maxine Walker serves as director of the Wesleyan Center for 21st-Century Studies and professor of literature at Point Loma Nazarene University in San Diego. To unwind, she paints small pieces of wood with folk art and weeds her garden while listening to country gospel and Orthodox troparion.

Jim Wilcox is an associate professor of writing at Southern Nazarene University in Bethany, Oklahoma. In his spare time, he can often be found standing on the corner of busy intersections holding a sign that reads, "Will write for food." He also enjoys singing falsetto solos at church and whistling Dixie.

INTRODUCTION

JIM HAMPTON

Each year hundreds of thousands of students leave the comfort and familiarity of homes to enter an unknown world —college. The fact that you're reading this book probably indicates that you're one of those students.

Leaving home for college can be intimidating. Messy roommates (or maybe a neat-freak roommate), leaving old friends, all-night study sessions, finding a new church home near campus—these thoughts can make even the most stout-hearted weak in the knees.

But think of what you'll be gaining: lifelong friends, the joy of learning and discovery, and the fulfillment that comes from preparing yourself spiritually to obey the call of God on your life.

The contributors to this book know what you're feeling. They felt this way, too, when they were college freshman wondering just what they were getting into. And they continue to encounter these emotions every fall when the freshman class arrives on campus.

Because they know the problems, challenges, and opportunities that come from attending college, they have pooled their collective wisdom to offer you inspiring and thought-provoking advice. Drawing upon Scripture, theology, and life experience, they offer sound guidance on how to navigate the college experience.

Don't try to read through this book in one sitting. Instead, read one chapter at a time, allowing the words to soak into and through you. Allow God to speak to you through these pages, and then put the suggested principles into practice.

College. Rather than feeling intimidated, commit today to explore the countless opportunities, and make these the best four (or five, or six!) years of your life. You'll be glad you did.

Part 1

THEOLOGY

If our anchor isn't set in a solid rock theology, we'll be washed out to sea on the riptide of bogus beliefs.

—Frank Moore

A LOVE THAT'S OUT OF THIS WORLD

KNOWING THAT GOD REALLY LOVES ME

GARY SIVEWRIGHT

AN EARLY LINDA RONSTADT SONG wailed that she had been cheated and mistreated and asked when she would be loved. Though I don't have the voice of Ronstadt, I understand the question. At the age of four I met the girl I wanted to marry. She was also four and was a newcomer to our neighborhood. My gang of friends and I were doing the things four-year-olds do—freeze tag, hide-and-go-seek, stealing hubcaps —when this girl came into my yard. She had the audacity to ask brazenly if she could play, but before I could say no, my friends were saying, "Sure."

Her name was Vivian, a skinny kid with long brown hair pulled back in a ponytail, big blue eyes, and dimples like crevices on both sides of her face. We ended up going to kindergarten together, then first, second, and third grades. During my fourth-grade year my family moved away. However, we returned halfway through my fifth-grade year. When you move in the middle of the school year, you know how the system works. You go to the principal's office where you are assigned to a teacher who assigns you to a desk.

Across the aisle from me was Vivian, still skinny with long brown hair pulled back in a ponytail. She still had big blue eyes and dimples like crevices on both sides of her face.

We started junior high school together. It was here I learned that seventh-grade boys can be put into embarrassing social situations often precipitated by well-meaning preachers' wives—like the Valentine's banquet the pastor's wife planned for our junior high teen Sunday school class. She announced that there would be good food and a great program—and then added, "Boys, you can't come unless you invite a girl."

I was like a deflated balloon. This banquet had so much potential until she laid on the big qualifier. Everybody knows that if you take a girl to a church banquet in junior high school, you'll be with her *for the rest of your life.* What was I to do?

Vivian. Skinny Vivian. I could take *her* to the church banquet.

The next day at school I explained my plight to Vivian. I told her about the banquet's good food and excellent program. I told her that if she didn't go with me I wouldn't be able to eat. As you can imagine, she was overwhelmed by that proposition. But she went anyway, and from that point on Vivian and I cut a deal. Anytime either one of us was in some embarrassing social situation where we needed a member of the opposite sex to accompany us, we wouldn't look for a guy or a girl—we'd look for each other. This worked throughout junior high and even into high school.

But in high school things changed. I started *enjoying* our times together. Vivian was the only girl with whom I was comfortable (remember that I had known her since she was four). We laughed, we joked—and she had changed. She still had that long brown hair pulled back in a ponytail, but I couldn't help but notice the hair swayed back and forth as she walked. Those blue eyes still took up most of her face, but those eyes could light up a room. And those deep dimples on both sides of her face were especially prevalent when she smiled—and she smiled a lot when she was around me. Last but not least, Vivian was no longer skinny. She had filled out, and—well, you get the picture.

I found myself thinking that this was a woman with whom I could spend the rest of my life. We had fun together, we liked each other, we were comfortable around each other, and even though she wasn't a Christian, I figured it was only a matter of time. We would graduate from high school and go to college. I would be a youth pastor, she would be a youth pastor's wife, and we would grow our own youth group. Everything would be perfect.

One night I walked Vivian to her front porch. The summer
breeze was blowing that ponytail, the moonlight was reflected
in her big blue eyes, and those dimples seemed to be saying
my name. I kissed her good night and turned to leave when
she called me back. "Gary," she said, "I never want to see you
again."

It's funny how your mind goes into neutral when it's blind-
sided, and I heard myself say something really stupid like "OK."

I'm not sure I ever really got over that 16-year-old heart-
break. Oh, there were others who shafted me, and I did my
own share of shafting. As I look back on the relationships of
life, including my Dad leaving home when I was in first grade,
every relationship seemed to add to my self-deprecation
whether I was the "shafter" or the "shaftee." It all begs the
question "If _____ [fill in the name of your ex-girlfriend,
ex-boyfriend, parent, or anyone else] can't love me, then how
can God love me?"

The Old Testament teaches that God is there for us. He
loves us enough to enter into our human dilemma. He faithfully loves us, and we learn about this love by putting our full
weight down onto His faithfulness. Isaiah 43 and Hosea 3 talk
about the depths of God's love relationship with His children.
We understand that unlike all other past relationships, love is
not something God is striving for. Love is not a heavenly ideal.
Love is the very *nature* of God. He doesn't just define the
word; He's the *source* of the word. So when Jesus came to
earth, the indefinable "agape" love that we hear preached
about so often today was demonstrated in bodily form.

Before Jesus, people would love out of debt, loyalty, or respect, but not often unconditionally. This "no strings attached,"
"say what you will," "do what you want," "my heart is yours"
type of love was demonstrated by God throughout Jewish history but was personified with Jesus hanging spread-eagle on a
cross between two thieves on a hill outside Jerusalem. By entering into a relationship with Jesus, as described in 1 John 4,
we discover the essence of really being loved.

She walked into my office, a college senior looking forward

to graduation. "You don't know me," she said.

"Yes, I do," said I, not really knowing what she meant.

"You don't know my story," said Kim, an attractive girl who could light up a room. She proceeded to tell me about her high school years.

She got involved with the wrong crowd and especially the wrong guy. When she got pregnant, she knew she had a problem. The pregnancy would be hard to keep secret from her very conservative, Bible-carrying, God-fearing mother. Knowing her mom would go ballistic, Kim told her the situation.

To her surprise, her mother remained calm and asked, "What are you going to do?"

Not being a Christian at the time and prone to making wrong choices, Kim said, "I want an abortion."

Instead of objecting, Kim said her mother accompanied her to the abortion clinic, praying and reading her Bible through the whole procedure. Later, as Kim turned her life over to Christ, she realized that the unconditional, nonjudgmental love of her parents, her church, and the Christian friends she met at a Christian college were the human affirmations of a God who had always loved her. As she sat in my office telling me this story, I could not help but remark how the love of God had transformed her countenance from that of a troubled, rebellious teen to that of a gracious, grateful, and very attractive young woman.

When my son was small and just learning to walk, he and I would play a game. Hearing the sound of my car in the driveway, he would run and hide at the end of the hallway. Waiting for me to climb the steps and turn toward him, he would jump out into the hall, bury his head, and run full-speed toward me, shouting, "Daddy, Daddy, Daddy, Daddy!" I often thought it would have been funny to step aside and watch Chad hit the wall at full speed. But I wouldn't do that to my son, because he's mine and he trusts me. When he came running to me out-of-control calling my name, I didn't take advantage of his trust and delight in his suffering. No, instead I picked him up and held him and told him how much I loved him.

Similarly, Jesus said, "Which of you fathers, if your son asks for a fish, will give him a snake instead? Or if he asks for an egg, will give him a scorpion? If you then, though you are evil, know how to give good gifts to your children, how much more will your Father in heaven give the Holy Spirit to those who ask him!" (Luke 11:11-13).

AND NOW A WORD FROM OUR SPONSOR

DEVELOPING A CHRISTIAN IDENTITY

JAN LANHAM

WHAT A PROCLAMATION! "You are a chosen people, a royal priesthood, a holy nation, a people belonging to God" (1 Peter 2:9). Yet many times as Christians we have trouble thinking of ourselves as a royal priesthood or a chosen people. Too often we find ourselves bound up with feelings of inadequacy and low self-esteem rather than confidently claiming our identity as God's sons and daughters.

Why is it sometimes so difficult to find our identity in God? Sometimes words from our past have obscured our vision of our true identity. As a college professor and a therapist, I've listened to countless people describe how words from the past have created scars and barriers that have made it difficult to hear those words of sonship or daughtership from a loving God. It's not a distant jump from hearing the words of others that declare, "You are disappointing, worthless, and inferior," to responding internally with "I am worthless and disappointing." Then it can be a short jump to the notion that God, too, must share these opinions. Why would God want me for a son or a daughter?

Words from our present can also quickly lift us up or dash us to the ground when we depend on the assessment of others to make us feel worthwhile. It's difficult to acknowledge our identity when our ears are tuned so finely to the whispers of assessment, approval, or disapproval from family, friends, teachers, or employers.

Our inability to live in the truth of our identity as loved children of God can paralyze our growth and can rob us of our ability to dream. How can we be open to ways in which God seeks to help us grow and serve when we're not even convinced that God can and will use us?

Low self-esteem can sabotage our relationships with God and with others. Sometimes low self-esteem prevents people from being honest, authentic, and vulnerable with God and with others. If only I could do this or if only I were that way, then I could be accepted and loved. So much bending and twisting to seek approval can cause us to lose touch with ourselves.

Some people struggle in finding their identity in God because they have not discovered the differences among inappropriate conceit, unnecessary self-deprecation, and a healthy sense of self-esteem. Sometimes at the base of prideful actions that alienate us from others is a nagging fear of inferiority. Any critical comments by others can be perceived as personal threats to one's sense of well-being. Walls begin to form that separate the inner feelings of insecurity from the images of competency one wants to project to the world.

On the other hand, in our attempts to avoid the trap of too much pride, which calls attention to our work in God, we can fall into the chasm of putting ourselves down, which denies our role in Kingdom work. Affirmations from others can cause us to respond with comments that minimize or dismiss compliments. "Oh, it was nothing." "I just got lucky." "Anyone could have done it." To continually put ourselves down denies God's gracious activity in our lives.

Our identity as God's sons and daughters calls us to the healthy acknowledgement of God's loving work in us. Yes, we have weaknesses, but we also have strengths. Our full growth depends on our willingness to recognize both aspects of ourselves. Our full growth depends on our courage to accept words of affirmation as well as words of instruction, guidance, and yes, even confrontation or criticism. In whatever circumstance we find ourselves, God's love for us is steadfast.

It is God who sets the expansive boundaries of our identity by calling us sons and daughters. It is God who reaches out to claim us as His own. It is God who wants us to respond to this call and to embrace our deepest and truest identity as the people of God. Healthy Christian self-esteem rests firmly on the foundation of knowing that God loves, accepts, and redeems us. His love is limitless. His grace is available to all who will respond.

While some people in our past and present have spoken words that deter us from claiming our identity, others have spoken healing words and have modeled lives reflecting God's gracious love. Their words, sometimes affirming, sometimes confronting, always point us back to God's outstretched arms.

It's also important to remember that we're works in progress. Many people confuse the call to Christian perfection with a false sense of perfectionism. The call to Christian perfection is a challenge to those who are sensitively listening to God's voice. Yet the subtle trap of false perfectionism has snared some into believing that it's their works, their perfection, that earns God's love and approval. This can lead to the uneasy feeling that we can never do enough or be good enough to please God. It's so easy, then, to transfer our own feelings of despair over our shortcomings and failures onto God and believe that He, too, is overwhelmed by our failures. We can never do enough to earn God's love, but that's precisely the wonderful truth of grace. Our responsibility is not to prove to God that we're worthy of His love; our privilege is to respond in love to the mercy, grace, and love already extended to us in Christ Jesus.

The God who created us knows better than we the nature of our journey. He knows where we need to grow, where our vulnerabilities lie, and where we're prone to fall. Yet He will always see through to our core identity that we're loved even when we feel unlovable or unloving, that we're accepted even when we feel unacceptable, that we're God's own even when we would settle for being orphans. Christian perfection is the journey of God working in and through us bringing us ever closer to His heart.

When we're able to embrace our identity as God's dearly

loved, we can take the next step of finding what our unique identity is in God. What captures your attention? What pursuits intrigue and engage your passionate interests? What strengths, abilities, talents, goals, and dreams have begun to grow in your life that God desires to coax into full blossom? If you set your mind free to imagine what God might accomplish through you as His vessel, where does your mind go? At the most practical level, when we can genuinely get our minds around the experience of God's love for us and our relationship as sons and daughters of the ever-living, ever-loving Creator, we can also face our shortcomings, our failures, our weaknesses, our strengths, our hopes, and our visions.

It's often the community of faith that helps us refine our understanding of our unique identity. The community can give us opportunities to test our interests and abilities. It can provide guidance and feedback as we sort through our options. Mentoring and accountability group experiences can be critically important in helping us fine-tune the paths we choose to pursue. Relationships such as these can provide resources for prayerful support, clarifying questions, and exploration of our vision for mission.

When Israel sent out 12 spies into Canaan, 10 came back and declared that the land was uninhabitable because the people were too strong and the cities were too fortified. Only Joshua and Caleb came back with a vision and an identity. They recognized that it was a good land, but more important, they were confident in their relationship with God, whose presence would lead them. When we can embrace our identity as loved children of God, we're set free to explore the many particular ways in which God gifts us not only with abilities but also with vision for our place in the Kingdom.

NOT MY WILL BUT YOURS

DISCOVERING GOD'S WILL FOR YOUR LIFE

Dean Blevins

WHEN A COLLEGE STUDENT approaches me with the question "What's God's will for my life?" there's usually a "story" behind the question.

- Perhaps the student bombed his or her first major college exam and wonders whether he or she should be there.
- Perhaps the student is at the end of college and now has to determine how to live in the "real world."
- Perhaps the student has been dumped by the person he or she was dating and wonders if there will be someone else. I once had a student ask, "Does God have only one girl in mind for my life, or is it more like a big backyard full of girls I can choose from?"
- Perhaps the student just got engaged, and the idea of marriage is terrifying.
- Perhaps the student has gone through a powerful worship experience and now feels called to dedicate his or her life in a new way.
- Perhaps the student is struggling in preparation for ministry and now wonders if indeed he or she is truly called to full-time service.

Whatever the circumstance, good or bad, the question is crucial. We are asking for insight into what gives our lives *meaning* and *purpose* in the sight of God. If Jesus is the Lord of our lives, we want to make sure we're moving in rhythm with His purposes.

Sometimes we use the language "Does God have a plan for

my life?" The question implies a predetermined, spiritual blueprint or map with every event already spread out before God. We assume our goal is to figure out the map and stay on course. I have problems with this approach, since it implies that God asks us to "guess" how we can follow the blueprint. We often base our answers upon a trial-and-error process, depending on how well or poorly events go in our lives. But good times may unexpectedly take a turn for the worse. Could God be playing games with us? Are the tough times actually bad or good for us? You begin to feel like calling the psychic hotline rather than living a Christian life. This line of thinking becomes frustrating, and I suspect God is much more forthcoming concerning what is expected of us.

The second problem with the idea of a predetermined "God's plan" is spiritual. If God already has a plan for our lives does this mean He has already decided whether I'll be saved or not? My understanding of the Bible and Christian faith says this cannot be so. God may intervene in our lives miraculously, but I can never believe God would purposefully design our destruction! Let's discard the notion of a blueprint.

So how do I know if it is God's will to stay in school, get a particular job, marry someone, or be called to ministry? If not a map, what is God's will for my life?

Scripture surprises us with the answer.

God's will is for your *salvation.* I'm always amazed by Jesus' declaration in John 6:33-59. The crowd came expecting Jesus to give them more bread for their daily lives. They were caught up in the day-to-day needs they faced. In a battle of wills, the people wanted Jesus to provide for their physical desires. Instead, Jesus reminded them that His purpose, His will, is actually to do the will of God the Father. The will of the Father, ultimately, is for eternal life for anyone who trusts in His Son. God's will for us, first and foremost, is not our material comfort but our eternal relationship with Christ.

We come to God with our circumstances and God says that we cannot know any more about His will for our lives without first accepting Christ by faith. You cannot ask what God's plan for your life is until you first find that life in God's story of redemption. This is not a sales pitch (such as "Believe in Jesus and then God will tell you what's important") but rather a matter of priorities. No matter what the immediate circumstance, God takes the long view—eternal life. We can celebrate that no matter what we face in this life, our eternal purpose is settled in our faith in Jesus Christ through the Holy Spirit (John 6:63). This is good news, particularly in a crazy, shifting world. We may feel completely out of sync with life, but eternity is a settled issue by God's grace and through our faith in Christ.

But if we're Christian and have thus settled the single most important question of our lives, how should we then live? If there's no blueprint, what does it mean to face each day with some assurance that we're doing God's will? This is the *real deal* when facing questions about work, study, relationships, and ministry.

The apostle Paul acknowledges that this is an important question and gives us the clues to daily living according to God's will. The first clue for me is in Rom. 12:1-2. Paul reminds us that living according to God's will requires discernment (testing and approving), which comes out of our daily practices (sacrifice and worship). Surprise! Instead of asking what God's will for *my* life is (where I focus on my circumstances first), I have to ask how *I* fit into *God's* will! We have to first consider what God is about before we focus on what we're to become! The only way we can know God's will is first to dedicate ourselves *to* God (becoming living sacrifices) by dedicating our lives *for* God and living worshipful lives.

Worship is always about focusing on God, sometimes through powerful experiences and sometimes through tough circumstances. Worship is a test of *discipline* in which we have to exercise our *will* to focus on God even if what we're experiencing is not all that great. Paul says we have to resist worldly standards and become transformed by a consistent renewal of our minds about God. Once the focus is upon God and not ourselves, we're in a place in which we can better understand what God has in mind for us.

The second clue comes from Ephesians 5:15-21. Paul again talks to us about living God's will (v. 17) in the context of worship (vv. 19-20). He also expands on this notion of daily worship, talking about our Christian conduct. We're to be wise, sober, Spirit-filled, thankful, self-submissive, and reverent. Paul is telling us that God's will for every Christian is to live a Christlike life, cultivating and living out virtues that are consistent with Jesus. The command is reinforced in 1 Thessalonians 4:1-12. Paul says we please God by living our lives as Jesus has instructed. We please God by not living our lives according to evil appetites. We please Him and are doing His will when we live sold-out and sanctified lives, holy and honorable to God. Doing God's will isn't following a particular blueprint but accepting a peculiar quality of life that says we will attempt to be Christlike in everything we do. When we stumble as we strive toward this goal, we can confess our shortcomings and move forward with a confidence of Christ's forgiveness and encouragement to live holy lives (1 John 1:9). We can celebrate that we don't have to guess whether there's a hidden agenda; we're doing God's will as long as we live our lives in a Christlike manner.

What's God's will for my life? How can I know I'm in God's will in my work, with my friends and those I love, and in my service to God? First and foremost, establish your faith in Christ. Make sure you've settled the eternal question through God's grace. Second, God's will is for us to worshipfully live our lives as radical Christians according to Jesus' life. So whether it's a bad test or a first job, can you rededicate your efforts as an act of worship for God? Whether it's a first date or wedding vows, can you live your life avoiding evil appetites and instead demonstrating holy and honorable actions? In whatever form of service you'll do, either as a full-time minister or a dedicated layperson in the church, will you serve in humility, reverence, and thankfulness to what God has called you to do? If so, you'll always be in God's will (Ephesians 3:14-21).

THE LEGEND OF MAE KUPPERMIND

MAKING DECISIONS THAT PLEASE GOD

TYLER BLAKE

HERE'S A TYPICAL DAY in the life of Mae Kuppermind. (Get it? Make up her mind?) She works at a big university delivering mail out of a pushcart. After finally deciding what to wear, she prays the following prayer: *God, should I ride my bike to work today or walk? Walking is better exercise—if I power walk— but if I bike, I'll have more energy to deliver the mail. What's Your will, dear Lord?*

If God doesn't give her an obvious sign, she drives her car. Once at work, another dilemma arises. While pushing the mail cart, she notices a piece of litter blowing across campus.

Lord, should I go over and pick up that candy wrapper that's blowing across the campus? Wouldn't You want me to take care of the earth that way? The trouble is, I'm supposed to be delivering the mail to the various offices on campus, and retrieving that wrapper will cause me to have to leave my cart full of mail unattended on this steep hill. What should I do, Father?

After work that night Mae goes to the pet store to pick out a new pet fish. "I've been praying for days about whether to go with the goldfish or the beta," she tells the salesperson, "and I just haven't heard for sure what the Lord wants me to do. I thought coming here today would clear things up, but it hasn't."

"Well, if it helps you any," the salesman says, "we sold out of betas this morning."

"Oh, wow!" Mae exclaims. "Is that a sign from God that I should buy the goldfish, or is the devil trying to trick me out of buying a beta, the kind of fish God has planned for me?"

Before she became a Christian, Mae had no trouble making

decisions. But now that she wants to do God's will, not hers, the decisions are much more difficult. *I can't take this anymore,* she thinks. *Finding God's will is too hard. And these are just the little decisions!*

Life is full of small decisions. And every now and then a big decision comes along. If you were Mae's friend, what would you say? She sincerely wants to know how to make decisions, big and small, that please God—so how does she do that?

The two obvious responses are to pray and read the Bible. Bring up decision-making in any Sunday School class, and those will be the first two suggestions. And, of course, those are both excellent ideas. But perhaps the *way* we pray and read the Bible has something to do with finding the answer. Let's take a look at these two ideas in depth, along with a concept that may or may not be mentioned in every Sunday School discussion of the subject—that of using the reasoning powers God gives each of us.

Prayer

You could say to Mae, "Just pray about it, Mae. God will help you." Mae's answer would no doubt be "I *have!* Lots! But I still don't know! God just hasn't given me a clear answer."

First of all, God cannot be manipulated. He is not like the Magic 8 Ball you ask a question of, turn over, and read the answer floating on a chunk of white plastic in blue water. We're not wizards who have His power at our disposal to use as we wish. God's perspective is unattainable by humans. We can't see things from every angle the way He does. If we could, we would understand why the answers don't come right away. Maybe He knows that we need to develop patience, or maybe He wants to see what decision we'll make on our own.

In any case, prayer is a daily discipline Christians follow in order to know Christ. It is not like an airbag in your mom's soccer van that you know is there but never use except in an emergency. If more Christians looked at prayer as a constant means of centering and focusing on God, they would worry less about how to make decisions because they would know God's will better—no matter what the situation.

Honestly, how do you start your day? By checking your E-mail or your favorite on-line bookmarks? Do you flip on the radio for an injection of pop culture? Do you turn on the television set and get a heavy dose of commercialism interspersed with the bad news of the day? Instead, try spending 5 or 10 minutes thanking God for all He has done for you before you even sit up in bed. As you see the effects of this, expand this time, and learn to sit quietly before the Lord for 30 minutes or so before you do anything else. You'll be amazed at the difference this makes on your outlook and your decision-making ability.

Scripture Reading

The other obvious vehicle to finding God's will is reading the Bible. This is always a good idea, of course. But as with prayer, *how* you read the Bible matters. Some people, when faced with a tough decision, use the Bible as they would the Magic 8 Ball. After a quick prayer to ask God to guide them to the right passage, they pop open the Bible (perhaps for the first time in a long time) and read the first verse or chapter they see. This reduces Christianity to superstitious wizardry. Nowhere in God's Word is this kind of reading suggested. What the Bible *is* for is to show us God and to enable us, through repeated study of His words, to be more like Him.

You see, lots of Christians believe reading the Bible is a great idea, but truth be known, they have read only small portions of it. How much of the Bible have *you* read? Do you read significant passages on a daily basis? If not, maybe a newer version would help. Paraphrases like *The Message* are as easy to read as your average dime store novel, but they still retain the powerful, timeless truths of God. Reading the Bible doesn't give you a rule for every situation you'll face in life. But it does give you principles upon which to base your life, a perspective to fall back on, and exposure to the heart of God so that you can reflect the wisdom that comes only from Him. Don't wait until you're in a predicament to read it—fill your mind with its wisdom now, and you will be able to make the right decision whenever the time comes.

Reason

Most Christians realize that sometimes, no matter how hard we pray about a decision or how much time we spend searching the Scriptures, the answer just doesn't seem clear. But have you ever wondered if this is God's way of allowing you the freedom to make your own decisions? Think about it. Your parents did their best to teach you to think for yourself. When you were a baby, they did everything for you. But when you're 40, will you be calling them to ask them if you should wear a T-shirt or a button-up shirt? OK, maybe once in a while, but every single day?

God gives us a mind for a reason. Otherwise, why would we need the ability to think for ourselves? The ability to use logic and reason doesn't come from the devil. God created it in each person. This is not to say that we shouldn't bother God with all our decisions. He cares about the very hairs on our heads, so much so that he has them numbered. But if you can't decide what do, use the reasoning ability God gave you. Try this: write down a list of 10 pros and cons, and then put a number beside each of these items 1-10, with 1 meaning "This isn't a very important factor" and 10 meaning "This factor is *huge*." Add up the two columns, and see which one has a higher score.

Instead of asking yourself if this is what God wants for you, ask, "Is there any obvious reason why God would not want me to do this?" If the thing you wish to do is not outside of God's moral boundaries, and if it makes sense, it's probably OK!

Finally, realize that God's love for you is unconditional. In other words, *relax*. We all make mistakes, big and small. The old dictum "Nobody's perfect" applies to everyone from you to your parents to your pastor all the way up to the highest governing officials of the church! Not one person has ever earned his or her way to heaven. The only people who have made it did so because God did them a gigantic favor and gave them the precious *gift* of salvation.

And as for decision-making, deciding to be grateful to God for His gift of salvation is one choice He cares desperately about. Compared to it, the rest is small potatoes.

WHAT COLOR ARE YOUR GOGGLES?
CHOOSING A CHRISTIAN WORLDVIEW
KIM FOLLIS

The hen is merely the egg's way of reproducing itself.
—Samuel Butler

NOTE TO SELF: Never borrow my brother's old ski equipment

When you're a novice to intermediate skier, only one part of skiing ultimately matters. I'm talking about that last 300 yards into the lift lineup. OK, maybe on the upper part of the hill you did only attempt the easy runs. Maybe you did look more like a newborn moose calf than an Olympic participant. But hey—once you emerge onto the runway into the lineup, who's to know you aren't busting up the moguls on the "Widow Maker"? Especially if you make a smooth, well-formed approach into the back of the line, culminating in a brisk skate stop that showers the last guy in line with a spray of Rocky Mountain powder. At that moment you slide up your goggles, exhale, and comment on the snow conditions with the casual air of an expert.

A few years back, I was enjoying an infrequent day on the slopes where I had just completed said moose calf impression and was in the midst of my grand entrance into the lineup. Unfortunately, certain conditions conspired against me. Large, swirling flakes of snow were bouncing off my goggles as I picked up speed over the last hundred yards. The goggles, as implied above, were loaners from my brother. The fact that they were somewhat scuffed and prone to fogging may have contributed to the mishap. The central problem with the goggles was the yellow tinting. You see, the thing about lift line-ups is that they use yellow nylon rope to organize the waiting skiers into rows. As I sped into the line with missile lock on the last skier in the inside lane, the rope was invisible to my blurred, yellow-tinted eyes. Just as I prepared for a knees-to-gether skate stop at the back of line, I discovered instanta-neously that between me and the chairlift was the yellow rope. Like a WWF wrestler, I catapulted off the rope straight toward the chairlift and tumbled down a set of stairs, coming to rest against a service door. As I looked up at the circle of faces above me, I came to terms with the fact that I would now stand in line with these people for the next 15 minutes.

What Color Are Your Lenses?

Reality is a funny thing. Everybody sees it differently. How we see things depends on the lenses we use to view the world.

We each see the world through tinted lenses. As with me in those goggles as I hurtled down the slope, the world takes on a certain hue. We describe positive people as those who see the world through "rose-colored glasses." It's important that we recognize that our lenses are tinted. Each of us tends to think that our view of the world is crystal clear.

One of the difficult things about college is coming to terms with the fact that your worldview is just one among many. Ski goggles come in shades other than yellow. I once took a col-lege English course taught by a Marxist. We read all of our lit-erature through the lens of class struggle. For instance, to my instructor Lady Macbeth symbolized the proletariat throwing off the yoke of the bourgeoisie. That class helped me realize that not everyone sees things my way.

Where Did You Get Your Worldview?

Your worldview lenses are a lot like my fateful ski goggles —borrowed. Parents, friends, teachers, movies, and books, among other things, all tint the way we interpret reality. Have you ever noticed that a group of junior high girls will share the same opinion on any number of topics? No one has to tell them if something is lame or cool; they just know. It's helpful to recognize the people and ideas that are shaping your worldview. Your gender, race, economic bracket, and region, just to name a few, are other contributing factors.

I am Canadian. Being a Canuck shapes my worldview. To me, Canadian bacon is just bacon and hockey is the greatest game in the world—at least in my worldview.

Shape Your Own Worldview

Going to college can seem a bit like the movie *The Truman Show*. In that movie, Jim Carrey plays Truman, who is the un-witting star of a TV drama that he thinks is actually his real life. His wife, friends, and coworkers are actors playing roles. One day Truman wakes up to the reality of his situation and then struggles to find his way to the outside world.

Like Truman, you're free to choose how you see the world. College is a great place to take stock of your worldview. You may find that, like my ski goggles, your worldview tinting is blinding you to certain realities. Changing how you view things is never easy. In the movie Truman had to fight his way out of the bubble.

How Do I Shape My Worldview?

Realize that, like Truman, you live in a bubble. There's a bigger divine reality out there that helps you interpret life. In his poem "In Memoriam," Tennyson is grieving the death of a close friend. At one point he breaks out of his earthly bubble and writes the following:

Our little systems have their day;
They have their day and cease to be;
They are but broken lights of thee,
And thou, O Lord, art more than they.

The Bible is really a window into the divine reality. In it we find men and women who were given a view of life outside the bubble. When they came back from the mountain, desert, threshing floor, Temple, or whatever place God chose to reveal himself, they had trouble explaining what they had seen to friends and neighbors. They were branded as plain irritating, lunatics, enemies of the state, or as saviors. Finally, divine reality penetrated the bubble in the form of Jesus. As the writer of John's Gospel explained it, "The Word became flesh and made his dwelling among us. We have seen his glory, the glory of the One and Only, who came from the Father, full of grace and truth" (1:14).

Just like the prophets who came before, Jesus was branded by some as plain irritating, by some as a lunatic, and by others as an enemy of the state. But there were a few, relatively just a few, who saw Him for who He is—the long-awaited Messiah come to save humanity from their sin.

As T. S. Eliot remarks in the *Four Quartets,* "Humankind cannot bear very much reality" (2nd ed. [London: Faber and Faber, 1959], 14). Yet reality in the form of grace and truth can certainly give life a clarity that can save us from the lift lineup ropes of life or a *Truman Show* bubble. How about those goggles anyway?

THE "JOY" OF SUFFERING

WHERE IS GOD WHEN SUFFERING AND EVIL OCCUR?

DIANE LECLERC

We always thank God for all of you, mentioning you in our prayers. We continually remember before our God and Father your work produced by faith, your labor prompted by love, and your endurance inspired by hope in our Lord Jesus Christ. For we know . . . that he has chosen you, because our gospel came to you not simply with words, but also with power, with the Holy Spirit and with deep conviction. You know how we lived among you for your sake. You became imitators of us and of the Lord; in spite of severe suffering, you welcomed the message with the joy given by the Holy Spirit (*1 Thessalonians 1:2-6*).

WHERE IS GOD WHEN SUFFERING AND EVIL OCCUR? This question has provoked much thought throughout the centuries. In fact, a whole field of theological inquiry, called "theodicy," is devoted to it. Another way of asking the question is "If God is God, then why doesn't He prevent suffering? If He's powerful enough but doesn't act, can He be truly good? If He *is* good but isn't powerful enough to act, is He God?" Although this seems like a lofty philosophical debate, it's not a question overlooked by Scripture. What is the message of Job? How are we to understand the persecutions of early Christians or the pain of persons who suffer innocently today at the hands of others? In the midst of tragedies, we have to ask, *Where is God?*

The basic answer to that question is this: God is with the sufferer. There is no dispute about this in the Bible. In this we find comfort, but we don't find the full answer to the theodicy question. I certainly won't be able to answer it here either. But I do want to reflect on a related topic a bit.

I have noticed how often Scripture links suffering with joy. Paul says to the Thessalonians, "In spite of severe suffering, you welcomed the message with the joy given by the Holy Spirit." And I feel my soul grasping to understand, not just intellectually but wholly, the relationship between these two realities—joy and suffering.

Don't get me wrong. It's not as if I haven't heard throughout most of my life some explanation of their relationship. But I must confess that I have found these explanations wholly unsatisfying.

Here's my problem—some Christians have implied that Christians don't suffer. For them, joy is the opposite of pain. And so they hold out the hope of wealth and health and a carefree existence. We can be joyous, they say, because suffering can be eliminated. But in reality, all we find here is a Christianized hedonism, where personal pleasure is the goal of the Christian life. This type of gospel preys on the sufferer and often results in disappointment and disillusionment.

Another explanation is much more subtle. Some people tell us that suffering can be, and even should be, joyous. But in my judgment, the ones who have claimed this have denied the significance of the suffering by saying that suffering really isn't that bad. But any sufferer who is honest about his or her suffering, when hearing that it should be joyous, must bury the pain or live in guilt for not being able to find suffering joyous when *apparently* others are able. Repression or guilt are the options when we say that suffering should be joyous. Dare I go so far as to say that claiming that suffering should be joyous borders on a Christianized masochism? Suffering in itself is *not* joyous.

Perhaps the most common answer, and the one that most tempts me, is this: joy can come in suffering because suffering has a purpose. Perhaps the purpose is to build my character or to teach me a lesson I need to learn or to make me more empathetic with those who suffer. But this viewpoint does not acknowledge that some suffering is pointless, senseless, and tragic from which nothing good comes. As a theologian whose job it is to make sense of these things, I acknowledge that this type of suffering keeps me up at night. I would absolutely love to be able to say that joy can come in suffering because all suffering has a purpose. But I can't. For to say this could imply that God causes suffering for a greater purpose. There are good Christian folks who believe strongly that God causes suffering as a part of His great plan, that in the end it will all make sense. But I can't. As a believer in the Wesleyan heritage, I believe that God can use anything for good, that He can bring joy out of suffering, but I can't affirm that God *causes* everything to happen. This would make God the author of evil. He can use suffering to teach me something to build my character. But if joy is dependent upon suffering that has been caused by God, I must bow out.

So I continue my search. How do I make sense of the juxtaposition of joy and suffering, so often found in the New Testament?

It helps me to understand that the opposite of joy is not pain but despair. Allow me to define despair theologically, primarily drawing upon the work of Søren Kierkegaard. Despair is not, for Kierkegaard, feelings of pain or grief at the loss of someone or something. Instead, despair is *utter and complete hopelessness.* He calls it the "sickness unto death." He takes the phrase from the story of Jesus raising Lazarus from the grave, when Jesus says this: "This sickness is not unto death." In other words, even in the few hours Lazarus is as dead as dead can be, Jesus says there is still hope. Despair is utter and complete hopelessness.

Suffering, pain, depression, and excruciating grief are not the opposite of joy. Despair, or hopelessness, is the opposite of joy. This tells me that in anything short of despair one can find potential for joy. This tells me that there can be joy in suffering. I don't need to deny the harsh realities of suffering in order to be joyous. I don't need to deny that suffering itself is painful in order to be joyous. I don't need to prove that suffering is meaningful in order to be joyous.

I can embrace suffering and embrace joy simultaneously and paradoxically. And I truly believe that this is a thoroughly Christian idea. I believe that the world cannot understand or make any sense of the fact that there can be real joy alongside genuine suffering. It makes no sense unless it's understood in the light of the Cross. The Cross was a place of defeat. In that moment the enemies had won, the Pharisees had succeeded in putting to death their blasphemer—the One who had threatened their very way of life.

And yet, paradoxically, the Cross is a symbol of victory for us. We say with Paul, "Where, O death, is your victory? Where, O death, is your sting?" (1 Corinthians 15:55). The Cross was a place of real, actual death. We embrace a Christ who actually died, who experienced real death. And yet, paradoxically, the Cross is a symbol of life to us. It was a place of intense, real, genuine pain and agony. We do not embrace a heretical, gnostic version of Christ, a Christ who had no body and therefore suffered no real bodily affliction. We embrace a Christ who took on brokenness in its most extreme form. We embrace a Christ who was really pierced, bled real blood, gasped for real air—a Christ whose body was truly broken.

However, to believers the Cross is a symbol of healing. It was a place of deep anguish and suffering, not just in body but in spirit, as Christ took on the sins of humanity, was abandoned by His disciples, and was forsaken by His Father. It was real in its emotional and spiritual suffering and agony. Yet it is today a symbol of great joy to us—and not only a symbol but also the source. The Cross is the source of our victory over sin, our eternal life, our healing, our hope. It is the source of our salvation and transformation, which mysteriously offers us joy in the midst of our own suffering. Where is God when suffering and evil occur? He is with us with the empathy that could come only from His own experience on the Cross, and that makes all the difference in the world.

Part 2

RELATIONSHIPS

We are, each of us, angels with only one wing, and we can only fly embracing each other.

—Luciano de Crescenzo

WITH A FRIEND
LIKE THIS . . .

CULTIVATING A
RELATIONSHIP WITH GOD

JIM WILCOX

> Your true identity is as a child of God. This is the identity
> you have to accept. Once you have claimed it and settle in
> it, you can live in a world that gives you much joy as well
> as pain. You can receive the praise as well as the blame that
> comes to you as an opportunity for strengthening your ba-
> sic identity, because the identity that makes you free is an-
> chored beyond all human praise and blame. You belong to
> God, and it is as a child of God that you are sent into the
> world (Henri J. M. Nouwen, *The Inner Voice of Love* [New
> York: Doubleday Publishers, 1996], 70).

PROBABLY THE CLOSEST FRIEND I'VE EVER HAD is my
old college roommate Al White. That's Dr. Villard Alan White
to you. He was, is, and will always be a whole lot smarter than
I. But for two years of our youth, we were peers at a small college in Nampa, Idaho, where we giggled our way through
classes and unrequited loves.

Al and I began to have lunch together once in a while,
where my single goal became to make him laugh with his
mouth full. (Unfortunately, I often succeeded when he was sitting directly across from me. Rice was the worst.) Sometimes I
would go up to his room on the second floor, and we'd talk
about girls, some of our courses, girls, our home state of Cali-
fornia, girls, music, and—did I mention girls?

When my first roommate dropped out after my first year
there, Al and I decided we were men enough to give living together a try. And for the next two years we talked for hours,

laughed for days, stayed up nights, pranked everyone we knew, and experimented with hairstyles, clothes combinations, study habits, phone voices, and waking-up techniques. We became "brothers."

It worked so well that when we took off for seminary after graduating, we roomed together again and even worked together. When he stood next to me at my wedding, he said it was "the death of his youth," and in our own way, I knew exactly what he meant: we had truly grown up together.

Let me tell you something—cultivating a relationship with the God of the universe is exactly the same process as developing a close relationship with a "brother" or "sister" here on earth. You meet through a mutual friend and start to spend time with one another, sharing similar interests, current hopes, and future dreams; learning to lean on and trust each other; and devoting a unique sense of loyalty to each other. You stand up with, for, and beside each other. You laugh together and sometimes cry together. You whisper to each other in church and yell at each other in your car. When his or her name comes up in conversation, you have nothing but positive, encouraging things to say. To talk about him or her is essentially to talk about yourself. You're that close.

It gets to the point that when someone sees you on campus or at the mall, he or she expects to see the other one not far away. "Hey, there's Al. Jim must be around here somewhere. Yeah—there he is."

Nobody, and I mean nobody, puts himself or herself between the two of you and lives to tell about it. For the first time in your life, you understand the scripture "Greater love has no one than this, that he lay down his life for his friends" (John 15:13).

A. J. Russell in his book *God Calling* (New York: Jove Books, 1978) provides a perfect outline of this process. He writes the "words of God": "Be calm. Never fear. Be glad all the time. Rejoice exceedingly. Joy in Me. Rest in Me. Never be afraid. Pray more. Do not be worried. I am thy helper" (27).

Be calm. Do not get worried.

It's amazing what happens when you start to see life and its expectations, interruptions, and setbacks through the telescope of eternal life. You begin to recognize your daily "crises" as mere speed bumps rather than brick walls.

If you want to get a sense of what a relationship with your Heavenly Father looks like, watch a six- or seven-year-old child. Better yet, recall what your own life was like at that age. You got up every morning with one thing on your mind: RECESS. Playing with your best friends was your No. 1 priority for the day. Chores at home were meaningless to you. Class work was simply a chance to rest a little before the next recess. Life was laughter, games, secret codes, tree houses, and jungle gyms.

And what made this play possible? What made you so content and confident? It was the recognition deep in your heart that all your needs would be met by the people who loved you more than anything else in the world: your mom and dad. They were not just working for a living—they were working for you. Their purpose was your happiness and health. They were your source of nourishment and safety. And when you went to bed at night with a full stomach and a soft pillow, you went right to sleep, because all was right with the world.

Never fear. Never be afraid.

I've been scared a lot in my life. Who hasn't? Like the late night in college when my buddies and I were pulled over by six cop cars, bullhorns blaring, guns drawn.

But nothing compares to the morning in first grade when a big, black, jaw-chomping, teeth-baring, drool-dripping dog chased me all the way to school. I was so frightened, I ran outside the crosswalk, earning an automatic appointment with the vice principal. Not until I made it to the sanctuary of the fenced-in playground and the familiar faces of my friends did I feel safe.

Think about this: God created the stars and skies, the waters and continents, the animals and trees. "Through him all things were made; without him nothing was made that has been made" (John 1:3). That same God created you and loves you more than all the rest of that stuff put together. And get this: His primary purpose today is your happiness. Knowing that, how can you or I possibly fear anything? Even big, black dogs!

Be glad all the time. Rejoice exceedingly.

If you listen to the 3,000 commercials you encounter today, you might think money will make you happy. Or maybe a new Trans Am or BMW. Or a closetful of GAP clothes.

That's a big bunch of hooey. American consumerism is based on the same principle as ocean water on a life raft. The more you drink, the thirstier you get.

No, wealth and creature comforts do not bring joy and gladness; as a matter of fact, materialism begets utter discontent and despair. (Just give yourself a few years. You'll learn.)

One of the happiest people I know is Paul Patrick. He and I have worked together for about 20 years, and I've never seen him when he wasn't smiling or laughing. He always seems to be driving in the slow lane, taking in the essence of being alive, serving someone in need, going out of his way to bring joy to others. He makes no more money than I do. He has one car that he and his wife share. He is nowhere close to being a Gucci/Armani/Rolex kind of guy. He's happy when his crew cut comes back in style every 30 years.

But when you talk to Paul, you get a sense that Jesus is standing next to him and the Holy Spirit is living within him. There's an assurance in Paul's demeanor that he has everything he could and will ever want or need: a family who loves him, a place to serve, and the hope of heaven one day. It's impossible to be around Paul without catching his contagious joy of living. He almost makes you think that Jesus wears a crew cut too.

Henri Nouwen writes,

The great challenge is faithfulness, which must be lived
in the choices of every moment. When your eating, drink-
ing, working, playing, speaking or writing is no longer for
the glory of God, you begin living for your own glory.
Then you separate yourself from God and do yourself
harm.

Every time you do something that comes from the
needs for acceptance, affirmation or affection, and every
time you do something that makes these needs grow, you
know that you are not with God. These needs will never be
satisfied; they will only increase when you yield to them.
But every time you do something for the glory of God, you
will know God's peace in your heart and find rest there
(*The Inner Voice of Love,* 23-24).

AN EXPRESSION OF GOD'S LOVE

MAKING AND KEEPING GOOD FRIENDS

DIANE LECLERC

> As God's chosen people, holy and dearly loved, clothe yourselves with compassion, kindness, humility, gentleness and patience. Bear with each other and forgive whatever grievances you may have against one another. Forgive as the Lord forgave you. And over all these virtues put on love, which binds them all together in perfect unity (*Colossians 3:12-14*).

ANN IS AN OUTGOING, SELF-CONFIDENT, engaging person who has dozens of friends. Kathleen is a quiet, reserved, cautious person who picks her friends with great care.

Ann enjoys socializing in large groups and loves meeting new people. Kathleen prefers low-key evenings with one or two close companions.

Ann wants to have as many friends as she can and cherishes the opportunity to know different people from a variety of backgrounds. Kathleen wants to know her few friends deeply.

If you were to ask either one of them, she would say that her friendships are a vitally important part of her life, even though those friendships might look very different. Our differing personalities might shape how we choose friends and spend time with them and what we value most in them, but it's rare to meet someone who doesn't want friends at all. Friends are God's gift to us in that He created us for relationships and for community. They're part of His design for us and an image of His likeness in us, evidence that we're social beings. Friends can provide encouragement and comfort; they help us rejoice in our successes and recover from our failures. They can spur us on spiritually, challenge us intellectually, and support us emotionally.

Developmental psychologist Erik Erikson has said that developing intimacy (and overcoming isolation) is the *primary task* during the stage of young adulthood. Intimacy takes effort. This is why many people struggle, rather intensely at times, with the question "How can I make and keep friends?" Although God created us as social beings, relationships are never (nor should they be) carefree.

I have great optimism that God can help us establish truly meaningful and lasting friendships. But I'm realistic and experienced enough to recognize that this does not always spontaneously happen. It is perhaps most important at this point to recognize that one of the greatest hindrances to good, healthy friendships is our own brokenness as individuals. All of us bring our history with us into our friendships—it's inevitable. Some of us have been wounded in relationships. We have been misunderstood, betrayed, or rejected by people we have trusted. Those on the shy side struggle under the weight of not being popular or not fitting in. Some are judged by how they look on the outside, never really given a chance to reveal their true selves. Worse yet, some of us find ourselves on a Christian campus where community is emphasized, yet we find ourselves terribly alone.

An awareness of my own brokenness is the first step in finding healing and wholeness, individually and relationally. Only God can really heal my wounds. I shouldn't look to others to do this work that only God can do. One of the quickest ways to ruin a friendship is to look to other persons to fill my inner longings and meet my deepest needs. Let's examine this further.

Perhaps I suffer from low self-esteem because I was abused or criticized harshly by my parents. But if I expect friends to be my source of self-esteem, I'll be crushed when they fail me. Perhaps I suffer from fear of abandonment because I come from a divorced home. But if I expect my friends to be there for me in all times in all circumstances, I'll be angry when they can't be. Perhaps I've never felt unconditionally loved. But if I depend on my friends' love and loyalty in unhealthful ways, I will feel rejected or betrayed when they don't meet my expectations. We must understand that friendships can never fill the hole inside us that only God can fill. I'm not saying that God can't use friendships in our healing process. But friends must be an expression of, never a substitute for, God's love and grace.

With these cautions in mind, what does a healthy, meaningful friendship look like?

Shared Interests

Although we can always develop friendships with those who are completely different from us, some sort of common ground helps give foundation to the relationship. Getting to know people from very diverse backgrounds, people with very different personalities, or people with very contrasting interests to our own can be new and exciting. But relationships built without some similarities seldom last. We often meet potential friends because we find ourselves in some sort of overlapping territory. On the other hand, as important as these shared interests initially are, we must also recognize that they're not enough to develop a lasting friendship. We've all had friends who are what I call "time and place" relationships. We share a job or a class or a neighborhood. But once the situation ends, we move in different directions. More is needed.

Commitment

There comes a time in every friendship, whether spoken or unspoken, when both persons recognize the value of the relationship. This sense of value brings with it a sense of commitment to the other person and to the development of the friendship. Commitment implies time spent together that's planned. It implies prioritizing such time. It implies investment that's intentional. Problems often arise when one person seems more committed than the other.

Reciprocity

No relationship will last indefinitely unless there is mutual commitment to the nurture of the friendship. There is potential for misunderstanding if one person is more invested in the relationship than the other. Have both persons owned the mutual responsibility required to make a friendship work and last? Are both initiating contact? Are both caring for the relationship? These are crucial questions to ask of one's more significant relationships. More casual friendships can exist without such mutuality. Deeper friendships will suffer unless the relationship is reciprocal.

Trustworthiness

Friendships are based on trust. At its foundation is the ability to hold confidences. We must seek out friends we believe to be trustworthy. And we must examine ourselves as well and ask whether we're trustworthy. But beyond confidences, trust in a friendship also implies a strong sense that the other person truly cares for us, will be there for us during difficult times, will honor and respect us, and will be loyal to us. We must ask ourselves the same questions: will we care, honor, respect, and be loyal to our friends? These actions do not happen by accident. We must commit ourselves to being trustworthy friends.

Authenticity

The value of authenticity cannot be overemphasized. Friends value who we really are and will attempt to provide the safety necessary for us to be deeply honest about ourselves, our pasts, our failures, our hopes, and our dreams. It's our job to provide that same sense of safety for our friends. Intimacy can overcome isolation only when we're truly authentic with each other.

Spiritual Nurture

Do our friends make us better people? Do we spur each other on in our Christian lives? Do we support each other? Do we pray for each other? Do we keep each other accountable? Do we bear each other's spiritual burdens? Do we rejoice in each other's victories? Christian friendship, in summary, should bring us closer to God. It should nurture us spiritually.

Virtue

A friendship is an expression of the Body of Christ, a microcosm of the Church. And so we owe to our friends the same love we owe to Christ's Body. We're to put on, as Paul says, compassion, kindness, humility, gentleness, patience, forgiveness, and love. Strong relationships are built on these virtues. Compassion and kindness will go far in providing a healthy atmosphere in which to grow the friendship. Patience will help us wait for the fruition of the other's dreams. Humility and gentleness will be necessary to nurture the other in failure. Forgiveness is crucial if a relationship is to last. Love, agape love, will bind Christian friends in perfect unity.

Both Ann and Kathleen, as different as they are, can achieve this kind of friendship. Not every friendship can be as deep as described here, but every friendship we have should be valued and nurtured, for every person is God's beloved creation. May we love each other as Christ first loved us. He calls us friends.

THE NEW RULES
KEEPING DATING RELATIONSHIPS PURE
GARY SIVEWRIGHT

IN THE THRILLER *The Sixth Sense,* an eight-year-old actor gained fame for just one line—"I see dead people." Those who have seen the movie know the premise that makes the line so important is that the dead don't know they're dead.

As a culture, we seem to be a society that's dead to sexual morality, but we don't know it. Sex in the marketplace has become so commonplace that we don't realize how dead we are to sexual purity. Your generation is surrounded by relationships based on sexual immorality. It shouldn't be a surprise that the comedy movie hit of the summer of 2001, *American Pie II,* was about the sexual prowess and dysfunction of three college-age men. And can anyone count the number of men whom Monica, Phoebe, and Rachel have slept with, or the number of women Chandler, Joey, and Ross have slept with in the years *Friends* has been on television? Surveys say a large majority of Americans today see absolutely nothing wrong with a person having sex with whomever and whenever they want.

The apostle Paul proved prophetic when he wrote, "Everything is permissible for me" (1 Corinthians 6:12). With these words he has tuned in to the mantra for today's generation: "I can do anything I want. I can think however I want to think. No one can tell me what's right or wrong for me." But Paul goes on to write, "'Everything is permissible for me'—but not everything is beneficial. . . . I will not be mastered by anything" (v. 12). The issue becomes freedom versus slavery as we deal with our own sexual urges within serious dating relationships.

I don't know if I heard correctly, but I think I heard a male college student pray at our chapel altar, "God, please take away my sex drive." Though I understand why a sincere seeker of God would pray such a prayer, I want to say this is a terrible prayer to pray. I certainly wouldn't want to be around if God would decide to answer it. The frustration for the young man should not be that he has a sex drive but rather knowing, as a Christian, what to do with it.

School begins, and across campus a freshman guy sees the most beautiful girl he has ever laid eyes on. About the same time, a freshman girl spots the most handsome guy she has ever seen. As it so happens, the two touch hands while reaching for the last chocolate frosted donut at the new student mixer during freshmen orientation. He says something clever like "Did you want that donut?"

She says something equally clever like, "No, you can have it" (while surreptitiously licking the chocolate frosting off her fingers).

The attraction is electric. Brought together by their mutual love for chocolate frosted donuts, they find themselves strangely drawn to each other.

What they are experiencing is what the Greeks termed *eros,* the passion that attracts us. It definitely gets our attention. But it's shallow, going no deeper than feelings and creature comfort. *Eros* might be a Greek word, but it isn't a New Testament word, because Jesus never came close to entering into a relationship based simply on feelings. You can imagine, then, how I feel as a college counselor when a young couple talks about marriage because of the way they "feel" about each other and all the things they "do" for each other. When "sharing" and "commitment" are not in the relationship, it's hard to imagine the possibility of a long-term friendship. However, once a couple learns the implications of *phileo* (shared, common-bond love) and *agape* (God-given, unconditional love), dating rules begin to make sense. As a youth pastor and college chaplain for the last 30 years, the following are the rules that I think apply to the young men and women who want purity in their dating relationship.

Rule 1: Never date a non-Christian.

Some people will make a case for "missionary dating," that is, dating for the sole purpose of leading a non-Christian partner to the Lord. I will not discount the possibility, but if I understand dating as a shared relationship that can lead to engagement and marriage, I would like to think that at the very beginning we could have a shared understanding of a value system that literally dictates every action of our lives. A non-Christian has no such understanding. In 30 years of ministry I have seen the Christian lead the non-Christian to Christ only once in such a relationship. However, I can tell you of dozens of Christian men and women who have had to make compromises in their own faith to keep the relationship together.

Rule 2: Watch no sexually explicit movies or videos.

I know it seems dogmatic in a day when sex is used to sell cars, jeans,.and diet cola, but I'm convinced that irreparable damage is done to a couple's relationship when they digest a steady stream of sexually suggestive material. I wish humans had the ability to always separate fantasy from real life and art from immorality, but the truth is that much of what we view becomes a part of who we are. If the eyes are the windows to our souls, then much of what we watch seriously affects our core values.

A group of social scientists found that a test group of high school students, after viewing three hours of MTV, had a seriously altered view of sex and violence. They discovered what many manufacturers already know about the unrealized effects of movies and video. Sponsors will pay for the privilege of "product placement"—that is, placing a product inconspicuously in a movie set so that it will be recognized. The manufacturer knows the identification of the product with the actors and the movie means bigger sales. And if a simple placement in a popular movie can encourage people to buy that product, then what about the *actions* of those actors? Do we not feel strangely compelled to at least give a try to the "What's it hurt?" "OK—for one night," or "Looks like fun" lifestyle of some of our favorite leading men and women? Values are easily warped by well-written, professionally acted scripts that mesmerize the most unsuspecting and play into the hands of the morally immature.

Rule 3: Do not compromise your own or each other's personhood.

What a woman wears (or doesn't wear) has a devastating effect on guys who are trying to keep their minds on purer things. Some women might be thinking men are perverts if they can't keep from staring where they shouldn't, but perversion is not the problem. Just the sight of things sexually stimulating causes men's minds to begin to race, and the woman becomes just an object. Guys become such an object when they become nothing more than a security blanket for a woman. It reminds me of the young lady who came to my office to excitedly announce her engagement. "But I have a question," she added.

"Sure," I replied. "What's the problem?"

"I think I can do better," she said, immediately calling attention to her reason for getting married—to have a husband, any husband. Some guys, knowing how susceptible women are to touch, gladly cuddle and kiss to fulfill their own sexual wants. When our actions with each other make us nothing more than objects used for sexual gratification, it *is* a perversion of God's creative plan for us.

Rule 4: What we do in secret probably cannot be good.

Time alone as a couple is asking for trouble. Our sexual drives are so strong that spending considerable time alone together is opening the door for sexual compromise. Innocent acts of cuddling, lingering kisses, and body massages are all foreplay to sexual intercourse, and any couple is fooling themselves if they think they're strong enough to stop before it's too late. Girls laying their heads in guys' laps and guys rubbing the thighs of their girlfriends are all preludes to an eventual sex act. If you think nothing is wrong with these last two innocent expressions of love, just ask the girl's dad if it would be OK for you to massage his daughter's thighs in front of him, and see what he says. It is best for a dating couple to keep their relationship open and public.

Hear the words of the apostle Paul:

Do you not know that your body is a temple of the Holy Spirit, who is in you, whom you have received from God? You are not your own; you were bought at a price. Therefore honor God with your body (1 Corinthians 6:19-20).

STUDENTS ARE *NOT* THE WEAKEST LINK!
DEVELOPING RELATIONSHIPS WITH YOUR PROFESSORS
MAXINE WALKER

HERE'S A TEST QUESTION: What are we told in the first few verses in the Gospel of Luke? If you're reading this during the Christmas season, you might think about the birth of John the Baptist or Mary visiting Elizabeth. However, what Luke tells us in the first verses is that he is writing this account to a young man named Theophilus—perhaps a university student like you. Luke writes,

> Many have undertaken to draw up an account of the things that have been fulfilled among us, just as they were handed down to us by those who from the first were eye-witnesses and servants of the word. Therefore, since I my-self have carefully investigated everything from the beginning, it seemed good also to me to write an orderly account for you, most excellent Theophilus, so that you may know the certainty of the things you have been taught *(1:1-4)*.

From a professor's point of view, this relationship between Luke and Theophilus is a good model for teachers and university students.

Servants of the Word handing it down to us

Many professors you will have in your university journey have chosen to spend their entire careers in this place. It's truly a sacred vocation—a calling—for them. Many believe that God directed them in their choice of academic area and in their selection of the university where they now teach. Many of your professors have made a covenant to teach as a part of their response to what God has done for them. Even in a secular university, your professors talk about commitment to a place that gives them wonderful opportunities to continue their studies. So when you choose to study well as a part of your response to what God has done for you, you're holding the baton that has been handed to you as you make the academic laps.

One of the greatest joys in my own professional life was to take the place of one of my favorite college professors when he retired and now to have colleagues in the literature department who were my students in freshman composition. As you begin your academic life, consider how God is calling you to study in order to "hand down the word" to others. Your professor is handing the baton to you!

Investigating everything carefully

University professors spend their academic life learning an academic subject in great depth. Professors who have earned an advanced degree such as a Ph.D. have spent years studying topics like naval history, quantum mechanics, Renaissance literature, genetics, or political theory—studies that put them in a rather small group of experts. You have now reached a point in your own academic career at which you are not required by law to attend school. You have *chosen* to study and to investigate all sorts of interesting things.

Learn from your professors how to investigate what you are studying. At the university where I teach we have a group of very talented science students who do research with their professors in the summer. Other students take courses to learn about college life or in an integrated semester to study literature and Bible or biology and sociology in a way that weaves the tapestry of learning together. Others travel with professors during semester breaks and in the summer. Traveling abroad is so exciting when a professor and a group of students explore the wonders of a Gothic cathedral or the Roman Colosseum.

In these courses of mutual discovery are times for coffee and conversation and times for praying and laughing. When I traveled in Hawaii with a group of students, we not only read important travel diaries from early missionaries and writers but also had picnics on the beach and studied the beatitudes in a local church.

"Investigation" means not only learning diligently in class and being serious about the various dimensions of the subject —even poetry and calculus—but also, as Luke says, investigating "everything" and "everyone" who encourages you to be a good Christian and a good student. That includes your professor!

Writing it out for you

Professors are really keen on writing stuff out. If you want to impress your professor, take notes. Luke wrote the gospel because he wanted the work of Christ to be remembered. On top of that, he wanted Theophilus to remember the correct order of what happened. This doesn't just mean that Theophilus would be able to perform well on a test but that these were some very important things for him to understand. Good professors encourage their students like that.

Most excellent Theophilus

As professors go, most aren't going to call you "excellent" —at least not the first week. You undoubtedly will not call your professors "your lordship" or "your ladyship" either. What the adjective "excellent" does suggest in a culture where we are usually just professor and student is the respect Luke has for Theophilus.

Most American college and university students have watched popular television shows such as *ER, Law & Order,* and *West Wing.* In addition to the entertaining dramatic plot twists, most shows usually include episodes that feature someone new to either the show or working as interns to the more experienced politicians, lawyers, and doctors. By the end of the show, the new doctor is wiser and more understanding of the patients and hospital politics. Sometimes the new guy on the block becomes a big star himself. Frasier started on *Cheers* with a bunch of just good buddies, and now he commands his own smash television show. Being "new" or a "novice" doesn't mean being unessential or insignificant. Consider that your professor thinks that you're definitely worth knowing!

So that you might know the truth

Truth is the heart of the whole academic enterprise in the university. When you were in elementary school, middle school, or even high school, you were learning the basics—how to read, what to read, how to calculate, and the basics of human civilization and the natural world. Professors now want you to take those basics and, with their guidance, start weaving materials into a whole piece. That is, you and your professors will be working together to make sense of raw data, to sort through evidence to decide what needs to be investigated further, and to trace how each academic area contributes to our understanding of the big picture. It's not just sociology and psychology that can tell us about women/men relationships, but also gender studies, poetry, art, drama, journalism, biology, and theology.

Professors have worked hard in their own studies to be prepared for your questions, doubts, and thoughts. They have wrestled themselves with how their subject fits into "telling the truth" about who we are. The best way to learn from your professor is to think about what he or she is saying and how that helps you understand Christ, who fully embodies truth.

About the things you have been taught

Whether obvious on the surface or not, love is involved in teaching and learning well. If we want to see the genuine article of love—the best of all in a relationship—we must keep in mind that we'll never see it all at once. Now that you're an adult, you can see love in the ordinary faithfulness of your parents, who, day after day, week in and week out, took you to baseball practice, piano lessons, or swimming lessons, or encouraged you to attend science camp.

When you come to the end of a routine lecture or even a tough exam, can you see the love in the eyes of your professor, who spends a lifetime in the classroom trying to instill in you and others a love for poetry, history, music, mathematics, chemistry, or theology?

It's easy to think of your professor only as one who gives either good or bad grades. It's equally easy to think of a student as one who receives either good or bad grades. What's more often the case is that the relationship between you and your professor is about being taught to live in love—not the soupy love of some popular songs and magazines—but love that asks you to grow. What you will do with what you have been taught gives meaning and significance for both you and your professor. Be like Luke and Theophilus!

FAMILY TIES

STAYING CONNECTED
TO YOUR FAMILY

Jan Lanham

"YOU KNOW, ONCE YOU LEFT FOR COLLEGE, you never really came back."

Spoken during a recent visit with my mother, the comment struck me that even though we are many years past that time, she still remembers that transition in both her life and mine. It's true. After college, I went on to graduate school pursuits and then marriage, and I never found it possible to come back home to live permanently. And yet we still feel deeply connected after all these years and have intentionally worked to keep it that way.

While you're in college now, how can you stay connected with your family while you're away? Even for those of you who may be living close to home while in college or are commuting to college, close connections are not the default setting. We have to work on them whether we're 20 or 50.

I've been thinking about this topic from the perspective of my own experience with my parents through my college years and also through the experience of currently having our oldest son in college.

Maybe the place to begin is to consider what your experience has been with your family up to this point. How close was your family connected through your childhood years? What was adolescence like for you? For some families it is a time of identifiable crisis and stress as the growing pains of the transition from adolescence into young adulthood begin to create points of friction between family members. For other families, the years go by fairly calmly with only minor bumps in the road.

What has your own experience been? If the past has been

stormy, is it still this way or has it begun to go more smoothly? Perhaps situations that occurred earlier need to be addressed in order for you to keep communication strong in
your college years and the years following. The college years
are extremely important developmentally. As you grow in your
understanding of yourself and your parents and siblings, there
may be times when issues of forgiveness, anger, or hurt need
to be addressed. Remember that the past does not necessarily
have to define what the relationship must be like in the future. From a different perspective, if your past was fairly calm,
it doesn't mean you can take your relationship with your parents for granted.

Have you taken the time to really know your parents? Do
you know what they think about issues? Do you know what
interests them? Do you know their likes and dislikes? Do you
know the ways in which you're similar to your parents as well
as the ways in which you're very different? One of the key
foundations for keeping connected is to really know those with
whom you're attempting to be connected. The process of understanding how your life has been interwoven into and influ-
enced by your own parents is one that will continue throughout your adulthood.

It's only been about two years since the death of my father.
As we came down to the last few days of his battle with cancer, I was extremely grateful that I was able to thank him for
the things he had given to me—his encouragement and support for all of my pursuits, his enjoyment of books and learning, his love for the ocean and his joy in sitting and watching
the waves roll in, his interest in people and his conversations
with them, and most important, his deep sense of the lifelong
strength that faith in God and a life intentionally lived in
God's grace can mean. These were gifts that he began giving to
me as a child. As I got older, particularly in adolescence and
college, I began to recognize these attributes as priceless gifts
to me, and both of us worked on staying connected through
the years.

We shared a love for reading. I would send him a book,

and before the next phone call or visit, he would have finished it, and we would talk about its contents. I miss our conversations greatly, and this reminds me that I cannot take my relationship with my mother for granted. I continue to work to stay connected with her.

I'm well aware that one of the important tasks of adolescence is the development of a sense of identity and an ability to separate from parents in a healthy way. This process leads to young adults who can lead independent, productive lives. It's not meant to encourage young adults to cut off their parents in ways that lead to disconnection and isolation.

In my classes with college students and in discussions with parents of college students, we'll look at the transition that occurs as adolescents move into young adulthood. It's the transforming of the parent-child relationship into an adult-to-adult relationship. Granted, you'll always be your parent's child, even when you yourself are a parent, but tremendous growth can take place in the relationship as you become an adult. Your parents begin to see you as an emerging adult who can take responsibility for plans and decisions, who has well-formed ideas and opinions, who can commit to new relationships, and who can follow through on spiritual commitments and spiritual growth. When this transition occurs, it's indeed an enormous one from the parent's point of view, because it represents the flowering of the years of emotional investment, nurturing guidance, prayers, encouragement, and support.

In the midst of all of the exciting things that are happening in your college experience, here are some things you can keep in mind to help you stay connected to your family.

- *Remember that you have a life outside of school.* Your family is still interested in what you're doing and in the growth in your life. Help them to know you better. What things are you learning about yourself that you can share with them? What are you thinking about in terms of careers or activities? Keep them current.
- *Ask questions about what is happening in your family's life as well.* Remember that your family's life still goes on even

when you are not there. What events are happening for them? What kinds of major decisions are going on at home? Keep current with life at home.

- *Show an interest in your parents' lives.* Know who they are. Do you share interests with each other? Are there ways in which your insights can be helpful to them?
- *When you come home to visit, take some time to be with your family.* Don't view the home simply as a place to sleep and eat. Remember that there are people there who want to be with you. Your parents are not simply running a bed-and-breakfast for you.
- *Be intentional about contacting home, whether it's through telephone, E-mail, instant messaging, or letters.* Don't simply rely on those at home to contact you. Of course, a balance needs to be struck here. While it may be great for the phone company, calling home every day can be indicative of a pattern of too much dependency that can inhibit growth. The key is to find ways to be purposefully connected on a regular basis. The means of communication are everywhere at your fingertips, but communication that connects lives takes intentional effort.
- *Remember, too, that you have a home church that would like to stay connected.* They still want to provide support and encouragement for you. Keep them apprised of your progress.

The college years are unlike any other time in your life. Never again will you be surrounded by so many peers with whom you can study, debate, discuss, encourage, and have fun. Never again will you have the coming-together of so many resources through the college faculty and staff at this important developmental transition of your life. Yet as you're growing, making decisions, changing, and maturing, make it a point to create opportunities to remain connected to your family who provided the foundation for where you are right now. This relationship is one that you'll take with you into the future as you move through adulthood.

LESSONS FROM THE WEAKEST LINK

BALANCING FREEDOM AND RESPONSIBILITY

KIM FOLLIS

REALITY TV IS THE LATEST NETWORK ATTEMPT to rescue prime time. One show that originated in England is a *Who Wants to Be a Millionaire?* and *Survivor* combination called *The Weakest Link.* Shows like *Fear Factor, The Great Race, Big Brother,* and others have found a following.

A recent search through some *The Weakest Link* web sites produced some interesting revelations. Is this a description of our collective conscience? Here are some comments from one site:

> The really, really bizarre thing about this show is Anne Robinson's no-nonsense attitude. We half expect her to take out a gun and shoot the losers (now there's an idea for a show!). The ultra-serious approach is certainly an interesting experiment and credit to them for trying.

> With Anne having an attitude like "You have banked $20. You could have won $1,000. That's pathetic," you as a viewer feel bad. Don't get us wrong—this kind of negative entertainment can be a perfectly valid objective for a TV show, but it does take a lot of getting used to. That said, once you've got over the first couple of episodes, she becomes really entertaining, and she's only saying out loud what we're actually thinking at home.

> Take this, for example. Let's imagine a show called "The Nicest Link." . . . Instead of "Well, team, in that round you banked a pathetic $50," we'll have "Well team, in that round you banked $50. Well done!" Instead of "You work

for an insurance company. How come you didn't know what 25 percent of 400 was?" it would be "Well, it looks like you got a question wrong." Instead of "Julia, in fact you were FAR worse than any other player in that round, but it's votes that count, and with four votes, Bob, you ARE the Weakest Link—goodbye," we'd instead get "Well, Bob, I'm afraid you've been voted off. Have you had a good day? Excellent. Let's give him a round of applause!"

Let's be honest: it's not as good is it? It's true that this show is a lot less so much about winning as not losing, and we know that's unpopular in some circles, but the fact is that the show is actually pretty compelling once the initial culture shock has worn off. (<www.qwertyuiop.co.uk/gs/atoz/programmes/w/weakest_link/index.htm>. Used with permission.)

OK—I know you're thinking, *So* The Weakest Link *is a sad commentary on human character. But I still don't get the connection between prime-time nastiness and my individual freedom.* Let's continue our search.

Is This Reality?

A recent winner on *Big Brother* lashed out at his fellow contestants. "Don't hate me," he said. "This is reality." Could it be that reality TV truly represents everyday life? Are we all watching our fantasy of the big score played out in a one-hour segment? Could it really be that if offered a big-enough prize we, too, would do what it takes to walk away the winner? Do we base our individual decisions on what will get us ahead of the pack? Let's examine how these questions and a reality TV show relate to the way you and I exercise freedom and responsibility.

The God of the Weakest Link

To God, it really is all about the weakest link. Let's give the weakest link concept a biblical twist.

God sent the prophet Amos a message for the people of Israel. "Hear this, you who trample the needy and do away with the poor of the land, saying, 'When will the New Moon be over that we may sell grain, and the Sabbath be ended that we may market wheat?'—skimping the measure, boosting the price and cheating with dishonest scales" (Amos 8:4-5).

What type of people do that sort of thing? Who takes advantage of the weak to serve their own selfish interests?

According to God, some good folks. The folks God condemns were highly successful people who were respectful of religion, even observing the holy days. They did all the right things in public, but according to God, they weren't as dedicated to Him as they were to their own greed. They were more interested in taking advantage of their fellow human beings than in living out the holy love of God.

We read something like this, and we want to say, "Well, that was a long time ago. Good people just don't do that sort of thing in modern times." I recently read a book titled *The Great Hunger.* It chronicles the Irish potato famine of 1845-49. What I found most amazing is the fact that while the Irish starved by the thousands, large quantities of food were shipped out of Ireland to England under armed guard.

England the good. England the Christian. An England reflected by reality TV.

"You are the weakest link—good-bye."

Freedom and Responsibility—Now That's Reality

One question nags me. If reality TV reflects "reality," what is it telling us about ourselves? I think reality TV is only telling us what we already know—we tend to look out for No. 1. In fact most of us excel at making sure that our circumstances come out right. Freedom can be interpreted as our right to look after No. 1. Certainly this is true in the world of reality TV. Every contestant seeks to come out on top, regardless of the pile of bodies they leave behind.

Into the midst of this "reality" comes God's Word. Listen to how the apostle Paul defines freedom:

Be careful, however, that the exercise of your freedom does not become a stumbling block to the weak. For if anyone with a weak conscience sees you who have this knowledge eating in an idol's temple, won't he be emboldened to eat what has been sacrificed to idols? So this weak brother, for whom Christ died, is destroyed by your knowledge. When you sin against your brothers in this way and wound their weak conscience, you sin against Christ. Therefore, if what I eat causes my brother to fall into sin, I will never eat meat again, so that I will not cause him to fall. . . .

"Everything is permissible"—but not everything is beneficial. "Everything is permissible"—but not everything is constructive. Nobody should seek his own good, but the good of others *(1 Corinthians 8:9-13; 10:23-24)*.

Paul understood what freedom was all about. He loved the freedom that came from being liberated from the bondage of sin. But he also understood that, as a Christian, he had a responsibility to exercise that freedom in such a way that he didn't hurt others in the process. He believed in this so strongly that he was willing to give up some of his freedoms if it meant that exercising those freedoms would cause others to stumble in their walk with God. From Paul's perspective, giving up this or that "freedom" meant nothing when compared with what Christ had already given up in order to save that person.

This is the biblical definition of freedom. It's always accompanied with a concern for others, especially those who may be the "weakest links" of society.

Our freedom means that we have a responsibility to choose. The question of freedom and responsibility is really a question of how we will respond to the weakest links in our lives. Freedom and responsibility are not about what we should or shouldn't do. They are about exercising our ability to affect the lives of weakest links either negatively or positively. The reality is that Jesus expects us to choose. There's no room on the fence.

What's Your Alliance?

We only have one real freedom—-the freedom to choose our alliance, that is, the freedom to choose between serving God and serving our own interests. Once we make that choice, then we're bound by the rules of our chosen master. What's the benefit of choosing your own self-interests? The benefit is—well, you've seen reality TV. An alliance with Jesus, on the other hand, means that we're now responsible to always seek the best for others, even the weakest links of our society. We always take into account the effect our actions have on others. When we look after others, we create a community where, rather than voting each other out, everyone gets voted in. Could this reality live in your residence and campus? It all depends on which alliance you choose to make.

Part 3

MINISTRY

If God goes anywhere this week, it will be our feet that carry Him. If God says anything to anyone, it will be with our mouths. If God touches anyone, it will be with our hands. And if He loves anyone, it will be with our hearts. We are the body of Christ.

—Karla Worley

GOD'S RESCUE SQUAD

HAVING A HEART FOR THE LOST

Elliot Johnson

Rescue those being led away to death; hold back those stag-
gering toward slaughter. If you say, "But we knew nothing
about this," does not he who weighs the heart perceive it?
Does not he who guards your life know it? Will he not repay
each person according to what he has done? (*Proverbs
24:11-12*).

MIKE AND MARTY PHELPS WORKED IN THE WOODS as
hard as they played football. They hunted and fished together,
played high school football in Pennsylvania, and then were
stars at Olivet Nazarene University. On August 12, 1993, the
twin brothers set out to hunt Dall sheep on Bernard Glacier in
Alaska, knowing that huge rams lived in the area. They had
arranged to be picked up 10 days later on a sandbar 20 miles
down the glacier.

As Mike and Marty passed through the rugged surroundings of Wrangle St. Elias National Park, they were awed by the
surroundings. Feeling independent, self-reliant, and carefree,
they hunted the drainage of the glacier, helping and encouraging each other as only brothers can do.

On the fourth day of the hunt, they quietly climbed into a
narrow, rugged valley. For three hours they crept slowly from
spot to spot, seeing several rams on the slopes. Jagged peaks
reached to the solid blue sky above the steep canyon walls of
ice and rock. They could see for miles. Suddenly came a small
breaking sound. Before either could speak, rocks and ice
blocks the size of cars rained down on them. Mike was pound-

ed flat, jammed into a small depression, but alive. Ten yards ahead of him, all was silent where he had last seen Marty.

Terror gripped Mike as he called out to his twin brother through the dark, frozen grave in which he found himself. Trapped in a bad dream, Mike struggled furiously against the frigid mountain that had engulfed him. Everything was blurry and in slow motion. After clawing for about 20 feet, he saw a ray of light. Cold and wet, Mike slid toward the opening and out into the brilliant sunlight—only to realize that he was alone. His frantic calls for Marty went unanswered.

Marty had been entombed in a frigid Alaskan avalanche. One moment he was full of energy and life, and the next moment he was gone. Though Mike tried desperately over the next several days to rescue his brother, it was hopeless. Marty's body was never found. Their reunion will have to wait until heaven.

Many of our friends and neighbors are in desperate need of spiritual rescue. They are lost in trespasses and sins and face an eternity of separation from God. All believers in Jesus are to be part of God's "rescue squad." You may not realize it, but you're the best one to reach some people with the good news of salvation in Jesus Christ. You have at least one friend who observes you for an example of Christianity. He or she is reading the book of your life and will respond to the words of your mouth. You'll be throwing a lifeline to your friend by living to please Jesus and using words that match your lifestyle.

Some people say, "I just live a good Christian life in front of others and let my deeds do the talking." It's absolutely essential to live as a Christian, but to never mention God's love and Jesus' death on the Cross and His resurrection is a cop-out. Many people will give the credit to you instead of God if you don't verbally point them to Jesus Christ.

One man came into the office on a Monday morning very excited about the past weekend. He began telling everyone how he had received Jesus as his personal Savior the previous day! During a break at the water cooler, a coworker said, "It's great you received Jesus. I'm a believer too. Now we can have a Bible study."

"You're a Christian?" asked the new convert in astonishment. "You were my biggest obstacle to receiving Jesus. You seemed to have life all together and you never mentioned Jesus Christ, so I thought I didn't need Him to get my life together either."

Proverbs 24:11-12 directs us to aggressively rescue those heading to slaughter. What better description is there of the unsaved? They are lost without Christ, and they face a dismal future. Psalm 82:4 tells us to "Rescue the weak and needy; deliver them from the hand of the wicked."

The faith of some Christians is weak. Maybe they're new in their walk of faith. Or maybe they've wandered away from a dynamic walk with the Lord Jesus Christ. Others may lack the confidence to explain the plan of salvation from Scripture. These are some reasons why Christians may keep silent about the hope they have found in Christ. May God help us to grow up in Him, to walk daily in His light, and to feed upon His Word!

Once God has rescued us from the penalty of our sin, He proceeds to rescue us from the power of our sin. For many, there is immediate deliverance from sins such as drunkenness, sexual promiscuity, gambling, vulgarity, and violence toward others. But for all of us, God daily changes our lives by changing our value systems and our worldview. We cannot remain the same as we were before He saved us. Ephesians 2:1-3 says, "As for you, you were dead in your transgressions and sins, in which you used to live when you followed the ways of this world and of the ruler of the kingdom of the air, the spirit who is now at work in those who are disobedient. All of us also lived among them at one time, gratifying the cravings of our sinful nature and following its desires and thoughts. Like the rest, we were by nature objects of wrath."

But Paul goes on in verses 4-5 to confirm, "But because of his great love for us, God, who is rich in mercy, made us alive with Christ even when we were dead in transgressions—it is by grace you have been saved."

We are now alive from the dead! Our attitudes are different. We are "clothed" with compassion, kindness, humility, gentleness, patience, forgiveness, love, peace, and thankfulness (Colossians 3:12-15). Our values become different as the joy of the Lord fills us. Our worldview changes from that of secular humanism to that of a Christ-centered perspective of history and the future. The Bible tells us of a powerful God who loved us enough to come to earth and take upon himself human form. Our new worldview touches every area of society as we conform to the image of Christ and see things as He sees them. We have a new purpose for living—the glory of God!

As we daily dwell on God's Word, we can encourage others. We can take others to a church where God is honored and His Word is believed and taught. Let us be loving and tactful and available to lift up, encourage, and pray for those who need Jesus.

God asks us to participate in the spiritual rescue of the lost. It's humanly impossible to save anyone, but God is able to do anything. He chooses to use us to accomplish the impossible. Be available to be used by God to rescue and disciple those who will come to Him for time and for eternity.

DOING IT

UNDERSTANDING GOD'S CALL ON MY LIFE

Maxine Walker

MANY OF YOU, even though you are just beginning your university life, are already very good at what you do. You may be a good skier, pianist, baseball player, jazz musician, soccer player, or published poet. You can testify to the nature of skiing by explaining how a person moves rhythmically and smoothly down a snow-covered slope. You can teach someone who has never skied to imagine what the cold snow feels like on a good downhill run, or you can suggest how to write poetry about the golden disk of the sun.

But there's nothing quite like actually skiing down the slope or feeling the hot sun strike your T-shirt on a summer day. This is not just talking about what you know but is about your own life and doing it.

Often students will view the university as a place where life is not really happening:

- "When I graduate, I'm going to spend more time doing church stuff."
- "When I have a family, I'll consider teaching a Sunday School class."
- "I was really blessed when I visited Mexico with my teen group, but I don't have the time to lead a Bible study for the Hispanics who work on campus."
- "Oh, sure, homeless people in my city need to meet Jesus, but I'm thinking more about a Work and Witness trip to Africa."

When I was in college, a special chapel speaker asked, "How many of you are thinking about Christian service?" Many hands went up. Next question: "How many of you have spent any time working in a church in the inner city with mothers and young children who are living in poverty?" Not many hands went up. Next question: "How many of you have ever prayed about being a minister in a church?" Again, many hands. Final question: "How many of you have ever considered what it means to be a 'minister' as a business major or as a philosophy major?" Again, very few hands went up, and frankly, as a literature major, I did not raise my hand either.

You see, the reason I didn't raise my hand was that I thought I understood that it was necessary for all believers to tell others about the fullness of God's healing and transforming love given in Jesus. But the truth was that I didn't understand that the more essential task to being a "minister" in my chosen field is to become the presence of God's love for others. What does this mean? It means not being set apart from others, not even in the areas where we're really doing the work that God has given us.

Teaching well is not enough; selling insurance ethically is not enough; running a cancer clinic is not enough. We're also called throughout our lives to be in the places where Christ would go and to talk the language of healing and wholeness that Christ talks. There are students in my own classes who need to hear about the love of Christ, there are women who clean my office, and there are professional colleagues who need to hear the word of hope as we rub elbows and chat by the coffeepot or make small talk near the broom closet.

Did you ever think about the shepherds and wise men who came to Christ's nativity cradle? They had lived their lives herding sheep and studying the stars—they were experts at what they did. Anything about sheep care or about reading the heavens—they could testify about that! If there were sheep-herding colleges or star-reading majors in ancient Bethlehem, these shepherds and wise men would have graduated from them. Now they were called to be new persons in Christ Jesus. What do you think this meant for them?

First, to have God's call on our lives is to use the gifts God has given us to move beyond our comfort zones. We are thrust out to those who differ from us, to those whose world is far removed from ours. Do you think the shepherds who saw the baby Jesus realized not only that herding sheep well is God's gift but also that speaking gentle words to their mothers-in-law is a calling of God? Do you think that the wise men who worshiped Christ with gold, frankincense, and myrrh realized not only that bringing the best offering is a gift to God but also that praying with their camel drivers who have no precious treasures is equally a calling of God? God's gifts enable us to bring God to others as agents of God's grace in a hurting and broken world.

Second, God's call on our lives keeps us from being phony and stale. If you're asked to pick out the champion from a group of tennis players sitting on the bench, you might pick the person who hasn't played in years. All of them have the tennis outfit, the right racket, the bottle of water, the canister of tennis balls, and the famous tennis shoes. But unless you see them play and sweat, you really don't know who is the champion. In our culture we love the image, and we often take on the values and perceptions that go with the image. Getting the right stuff for the image becomes a cocoon that protects us from getting sweaty in the kingdom of God. A life lived under the Holy Spirit's guidance is like figuring out the champion player—what's the real thing!

Understanding the call of God throughout life also keeps us yearning for wholeness and completion that can come only from the work of the Holy Spirit. Our lives are marked by finishing what we start: finishing school to get a diploma; finishing dating to get married; finishing an internship to get a promotion; finishing a year of work to get a vacation. There's always a slight sadness when we finish something—friends go their separate ways after graduation; we move away from parents and siblings when we marry; vacations must come to an end. God's call on our lives is the ongoing call and longing for wholeness throughout. We're not done until the end of life itself!

When we come to understand that our lives are animated by God, who "fills all in all," our ministry has no end. John

Wesley, the 18th-century minister and founder of Methodism, likened our spiritual journey in grace to a baby growing. Is an eight-month-old baby inferior to an 80-year-old? Is a 9th grader inferior to a 12th grader? No! Our growth, our experiences, our learning, our perceptions, our abilities, and our gifts are appropriate to our age and to our development as human beings.

So it is with us Christians. Each stage of life becomes a promise and joyous opportunity to be filled with the Spirit, who leads us into unique ways to grow and to serve.

FROM OUR HEARTS TO OUR HANDS

DEVELOPING A COMPASSIONATE LIFESTYLE

Diane Leclerc

> On one occasion an expert in the law stood up to test Jesus. "Teacher," he asked, "what must I do to inherit eternal life?" "What is written in the law?" [Jesus] replied. . . . He answered: "'Love the Lord your God with all you heart and with all your soul and with all your strength and with all your mind'; and, 'Love your neighbor as yourself.'" "You have answered correctly," Jesus replied. "Do this and you will live." But he wanted to justify himself, so he asked Jesus, "And who is my neighbor?" (Luke 10:25-29).

WE KNOW THE SCENARIO that prompts Jesus to tell the well-known parable of the Good Samaritan—the religious experts are at it again. We know that they keep trying to get at Jesus, trying to corner Him, trying to trip Him up, trying to wear Him down, trying to get Him to crack under the pressure and reveal himself as an impostor. And now, this particular man—who, our passage tells us, is desperately trying to find a loophole to justify himself—is the one who finds himself with no excuse in the end as Jesus tells the powerful and penetrating parable of the Good Samaritan.

In this parable it's the religious men who fail miserably, who, when all is said and done, end up looking like fools. And interestingly, certainly not coincidentally, the religious men in the parable happen to look very much like the religious experts who come to question Jesus. Jesus makes His point. And we get a glimpse of what the writer of Hebrews means when he says that the word of God divides bone from marrow like a double-edged sword.

But there is more for us to do than just cheer the Good Samaritan from the sidelines. Scripture invites us in. We are a part of the story. Each of us can be seen in this parable, too, and it's our task to decide which character in the story best represents us. Which character represents you?

Compassion is a word we throw around a lot, and we probably have some understanding of what it means. Beyond sheer definition, we've probably experienced it. If I begin to tell you the stories of persons I know, I believe you would begin to feel the internal tugging on your hearts that we most often label as compassion. I could tell you about Liz, who had an alcoholic father and a schizophrenic mother and was raised by five different foster families, the last of which used the foster money to get drunk every night. I could tell you about Joan, who after raising a family as best she could, now finds herself as one of a growing statistic, an elderly woman regularly beaten by her own daughter. I could tell you countless stories of other people's innocent suffering. We feel for the people in situations like these. We may feel pity or sympathy or even empathy.

But we must not mistake these feelings for compassion. Compassion is certainly a feeling, but it's also much more. It's action. Compassion is being moved by one's heart to act. The Good Samaritan showed compassion because he not only felt pity for the fallen man (which our text tells us he did, in fact, feel) but also *acted* on that pity, entering into this person's suffering, acting to bring restoration and healing. He did not think about the cost to himself; he did not consider how this guy was going to repay him for his kindness. He simply acted—with no regard for himself. He was concerned only about what the fallen one needed. He was truly compassionate—he acted.

Who best represents you in the parable? This is where most reflections on this parable contrast the priest and the Levite with the Good Samaritan. This is where some expositions make us feel guilty for being like the priest and the Levite and use that guilt to motivate us into being nicer to people. Who best repre-

sents you in this parable? Before you ponder that too long, I
want to make a suggestion: that Jesus himself is the Good
Samaritan. He did not give us an example that He did not follow
himself. Jesus Christ did not consider the cost to himself when
He died on the Cross; He did not and does not think about how
we are going to repay Him—we cannot repay Jesus, only thank
Him. Jesus himself is the Good Samaritan. And if it's appropriate
to see Him as the Good Samaritan, then who are we?

I would like to propose this: We, you and I, are the fallen
ones who are left to die unless someone saves us. We're the
fallen ones in desperate need for someone to rescue us. We're
the fallen ones who have wounds we can't bind up ourselves.
We're the fallen ones in need of restoration, healing, compassion, and love. We're the fallen ones, beaten up, wounded,
bleeding, dying. And Jesus Christ is our Good Samaritan. God
did not simply look down at our fallen condition and feel for
us. He acted. He had compassion on us and sent Jesus Christ
to bring healing and salvation. Out of that compassion, Christ
died for you and me. He acted.

How can we, then, develop a compassionate lifestyle? First
and foremost, we must experience the compassion of God toward us. It's only out of our own sense that we've been greatly
loved that we find in ourselves the capacity to love greatly. In
other words, "Freely you have received. Freely give."

If we read Scripture closely, we will see this message
throughout. We are to show love because we have been loved.
We are to show grace because we have been graced. The very
covenant itself involved a promise conjoined with responsibility. God blessed Israel, so that they might be a blessing to other nations. Isaiah says, "Is not this the kind of fasting I [the
Lord] have chosen: to loose the chains of injustice and untie
the cords of the yoke, to set the oppressed free and break
every yoke? Is it not to share your food with the hungry and
to provide the poor wanderer with shelter?" (58:6-7). Hosea,
loved by God, was to act like God in his acceptance and faithfulness to an adulterous wife. Judgment would fall on Israel,
according to Amos, because they had "trampled on the heads

of the poor" (2:7). Blessed are the meek, the merciful, and the peacemakers, Matthew records in chapter 5. John spends an entire letter on the theme of this verse—"since God so loved us, we also ought to love one another" (1 John 4:11). In Romans 12, Paul admonishes that "in view of God's mercy," we're to offer ourselves as "living sacrifices" (v. 1) and to bless those who persecute us. He then ends the chapter, in verse 20, by quoting from Proverbs: "If your enemy is hungry feed him; if he is thirsty, give him something to drink." James goes so far as to say, "Religion that God our Father accepts as pure and faultless is this: to look after orphans and widows in their distress" (1:27). This is only a glimpse into a primary theme of the Scriptures. None of this is possible without compassion. But compassion is impossible without truly receiving, in the depths of our being, the transforming love of God.

And yet God, because of His great compassion for us and His desire that we seek His ways freely, never coerces us into following His intentions. While grace enables us to live a life of love, it never forces us to do so. We, then, must intentionally cooperate. His will empowers us, but we must act. We must decide, in the spirit of the Good Samaritan, to bend to help the fallen ones in their distress. We must act. Compassion flows outward from our hearts *to our hands.*

AN ATTITUDE OF GRATITUDE AND FAITHFULNESS

BEING INVOLVED IN THE LOCAL CHURCH

Dean Blevins

COLLEGE LIFE BRINGS a whole new sense of freedom and choice. Freedom is a wonderful thing when we make sound choices. One key decision for us as Christians revolves around why we should participate in a local church.

Traditionally, people will try to convince us to be involved in the local church by volunteering our time, saying that our participation will be both enjoyable and enriching. They say, "Just spend your time with us and you'll be happier, and your ministry will make a difference." We hear about how much good we can do and how much good our participation will do for us and for others. In many respects this invitation is true —church can be a place where we benefit from our associations and our service. We can find our lives richer and more enjoyable not only in attending but also by helping others through the church.

Sunday mornings, however, often become a balancing act —weighing whether we gain more by attending church or by choosing to sleep in. Balancing our freedom with personal gain gets us into trouble. There must be more to motivate our involvement in church.

If I believe the traditional invitation, then I go to church voluntarily because I'll get something out of my attendance. Church begins to sound like a spectator sport. This becomes dangerous language, implying that everything is determined by how *I* spend *my* time and efforts. Believing this sales pitch

risks reducing the best of our lives to a type of economic exchange. Our time and efforts are our possessions. We spend
our time or our abilities and, in exchange, purchase happiness, success, or well-being—all based on our "investment" in
the Church. The Church and our participation in it sound
more like an infomercial.

Sometimes when asked to do something really difficult or
courageous for the Church, we shy away. None of us is, after
all, Billy Graham, Mother Theresa, or John Wesley. Therefore,
we decline because we don't have abilities to match what other
people can do. The more we buy into this way of thinking, the
more we begin to feel as if everything in our personal lives, including our activities in the local church, resembles a giant au-
tomated teller machine. We limit our involvement because we
have just so much time and energy we can spend with what we
have. This view of reality reduces our personal lives to some
kind of bank statement. Is this a good motivation for attending
and serving in and through the church? To be honest, is this
what *life* is about? There has to be another way.

When we turn to the stories of others involved in and
through church, we're surprised that God works by a different
set of motivations. When the Holy Spirit exploded upon the
people in the Upper Room with rushing wind and flame, as
described in Acts 2, people immediately came together to see
what was happening. Peter preached, the people responded,
and another new community—the Church—was born. Some
might like to think it was Peter's eloquent sales speech that at-
tracted the converts, but it doesn't take long to realize that it
was the power of the Holy Spirit working in people to bring
them to repentance—and to bring them together. The Book of
Acts teaches us that God creates the Church through the power of the Holy Spirit. God's redeeming relationship saved people who were grateful to enter into a new life. People gathered
together and ministered out of a sense of *gratitude* and *obedience* to God. These two attitudes should shape our lives in the
Church today.

The individuals who made up the Early Church described in

Acts 2 knew this as well. They gathered together to praise, break bread, and "give thanks" in worship to the God that graciously redeemed them. They also gathered to learn deeply of their new life in Christ, to care for one another, to eat together in honest fellowship, to serve their world in humility, and to tell the Good News so others could respond to Christ. "Individual" or "volunteer" Christianity was not an option. People who accepted Christ in a personal sense were immediately ushered into a new community, a new way of living and loving together. Our new humanity is born again in our relationships with Jesus and with other believers. In the economics of God's grace, we gather as authentic human beings, not potential bank statements or credit cards, because we have already received more than we could ever earn, and we want to give it away to others.

Gratitude should be enough, but we must remember that these church practices were also done out of obedience. Christians gathered not because they always felt like it, but because the Lord commanded it. Frankly, Acts 5 tells the story of two people, Ananias and Sapphira, who thought they could turn their relationships with the Church into an economic exchange such as we earlier discussed. It cost them their lives. We may have a hard time with this story, but the shock of the account is straightforward: anytime we think we can barter our relationship with Christ's community, the Church, we're on dangerous ground. We do not own God's creation, the Church. We do not buy into God's Church, but we obediently become the people of God. The church becomes the place that holds us accountable to God.

New Testament Christians lived obediently, because God has always called a community to be His people. Just as Moses came down from Sinai to take a motley crew of people and turn them into the nation of Israel, the apostles did the same for the Church. In several letters, Paul calls Christians participating in churches "saints." Paul does not think of them as individualistic folk who happen to be in one congregation. Instead, he sees them as a people who collectively love, worship, serve, and witness in obedience and faithfulness.

I believe the true saints of the Church know this. Can I tell you a secret? Mother Theresa, Billy Graham, and John Wesley did not start out to be "successful" Christians—just faithful ones. They had no aspirations of fame—only a desire to serve the Church in the best way they could. Most people who rise to greatness in the Christian faith do so out of obedience and accountability during difficult times. Those who participate only so they can be noticed often disappear during those tough yet crucial moments. Some of the greatest failures of Christian history were the result of talented but self-absorbed Christians. God does not call us to successes but rather to be faithful in our service to Christ through the Church.

I would advise you to seek activities that both express your gratitude and deepen your faithfulness. You can express your gratitude through worship. Direct praise of God is a primary response to God's grace. When we prepare ourselves to worship, not to gain but to give ourselves, we become lost in God's overflowing love. John Wesley defined worship as "spiritual respiration." As we exhale praise, we then inhale the Spirit of God and all the grace possible. Faithfulness, or obedience, can be expressed through discipleship. Faithful discipleship shapes us into Christian maturity by disciplining our practices of faith through prayer, fasting, Scripture-reading, and righteous living. This discipleship deepens as we allow our Christian lives to be challenged and encouraged by others, becoming accountable to a group of like-minded Christians who seek Christlikeness.

Gratitude and obedience, however, are also expressed in service, witness, and compassion, both within the congregation and through the Church to the world. Serving others, ministering to people in the name of Christ, is a way of demonstrating our gratitude. It provides an opportunity to extend the grace of God to others. Servanthood also expresses faithfulness. When we obediently reach out to others, we're surprised how often we discover Jesus at work through the people we serve.

Why should you become involved in a church? If you're a

Christian, the answer is clear. A Christian without a church is like a fish without water. We become involved first out of a sense of gratitude—God loves us, redeems us, and calls us to community. We also become involved out of a sense of obedience and the need for a community in which to practice and proclaim our faith. Instead, ask yourself this question: "How can I express my gratitude and obedience to Christ through my involvement in *this* church?" Seek to find ways not only to attend a church but also to respond through deliberate involvement. Once we get the question right, the answer will be easy to find.

WRAP A TOWEL AROUND YOUR WAIST

SEEING YOUR CAMPUS AS A MINISTRY OPPORTUNITY

Gary Sivewright

FIRST PETER 4:7 READS, "The end of all things is near"—an interesting idea in that it was written almost 2,000 years ago. I'm sure every Christian who lived about the time of Christ hoped that Jesus would return soon, but it was not to be. Jesus' return is not the essence of this passage, just as "Maranatha," "Come, Lord," was not the message of the New Testament Church. So note what Peter says next:

Therefore, be clear minded and self-controlled so that you can pray. Above all, love each other deeply, because love covers over a multitude of sins. Offer hospitality to one another without grumbling. Each one should use whatever gift he has received to serve others, faithfully administering God's grace in its various forms. If anyone speaks, he should do it as one speaking the very words of God. If anyone serves, he should do it with the strength God provides, so that in all things God may be praised through Jesus Christ. To him be the glory and the power for ever and ever. Amen *(1 Peter 4:7-11)*.

The message of the New Testament Church, and still the message today, is "He's alive!" While we await the return of Christ, whenever that might be, let's get on with the *work* of Christ. When Jesus returns, let Him find us doing what He would do if He were on earth. This is the work of the Church, the "body of Christ" (Ephesians 4; 1 Corinthians 12). I believe this is a literal picture for the apostle. Jesus is the head, the

90

brains, the control center, and the believers are the various parts of the Body carrying out the work.

Let's say I'm playing basketball in the gym. I'm doing my patented 360° slam dunks, and guys 30 years my junior are jealous. They must stop me. As I put the blindfold on for my last dunk, the boys dream up a plan. When I leap for the basket, the gang swipes my legs out from under me. My leg hits the floor, my knee scrapes the wood, and the skin on my knee splits. Immediately my brain goes into action. It tells my eyes to go into a crazed expression; it tells my mouth and vocal chords to yell for an ambulance; it tells my hands and arms to go down to where the cut is; it tells my entire body to flop around on the ground. On the inside of my body, other things are happening. My brain tells my platelets to go down to the cut and clot. What would happen if my platelets said, "No, we don't want to." Brain would say, "You don't understand. Clotting is your job. Get down there and clot." And the platelets would say, "No. We've clotted for the last time. This jerk falls down every time he plays basketball. We're not clotting." And so I end up bleeding to death on the court.

"Ridiculous," you say. "A body doesn't turn on itself." A *sick* body does. God has given each of us gifts with which to encourage and build each other up. These gifts can be the obvious—preaching, teaching, witnessing, and so on. Or they can be gifts not so obvious but no less important. I believe there are gifts like caring, believing, listening, and loving.

This ministry is not for the future. It's not for just the super talented. It's for the present, and it's for all who call themselves Christian. We are not the Body of Christ because we look alike, think alike, and act alike. We don't agree on everything. As believers we have only one thing in common—the love of Christ. It's this love that makes us one. Just as blood is the life-flow of the physical body that brings life into every part, so is Christ's love the life-flow of the spiritual body.

What if one of God's anointed decided they would not give anymore? Maybe that person is tired of being taken advantage of. Perhaps he or she doesn't like the direction the rest of the

Church is going. So the person pulls himself or herself out, albeit temporarily, from ministry within the Body. My son Chad experienced a blood disorder as a child called idiopathic thrombosylopenia purpura (ITP). This disease mysteriously comes and initially looks much like leukemia, though it's not nearly as dangerous. But when Chad had ITP, he was a bleeder. If he got cut, we would have to go to the hospital to stop the bleeding. If he got hit in the head, there was the possibility of a cerebral hemorrhage that could kill him. We came to understand how serious it is when the human body is not functioning the way it should. It's the same way on any Christian college campus. Surrounded by those whom the Holy Spirit has anointed to minister with various gifts, if it does not happen, the campus community is sick and eventually dies spiritually.

Peter had to learn this the hard way. When Jesus died, Peter was disillusioned. Like many zealous Jews, he was convinced the Messiah would aid in the overthrow of the Roman Empire. He waited for Jesus to return the Jews to their rightful place of authority. But when Jesus hung spread-eagle between two thieves at the town trash heap, the dream was over. The bubble had burst. Peter went back to the life he had known when Jesus found him: fishing. As Peter and his friends were pulling an all-night fishing trip, a voice yelled from the shore, "Are you catching anything?" "No," they replied. "Then throw your net on the other side of the boat." And to their amazement, fish started jumping into the net. Big fish. Celebrity fish. Charlie the Tuna, Shamu, Jaws—the net was full. Peter took another look at the figure on shore and recognized Jesus. He threw on his shirt, jumped overboard, and swam to where Jesus was standing. Jesus called Peter aside and asked, "Do you love me?"

It is difficult to understand what is going on between this teacher and His student. When Jesus uses the "love" word, He's saying *agapē*, an almost untranslatable word in Jesus' time in that it means an unconditional, laying-down-your-life kind of love. No one loved that devotedly until Jesus.

Peter responded, "Lord, you know I'm your friend," but was not able to respond on the same level of love that Christ was asking. So Jesus approached it another way: "If you're my friend, you'll feed my sheep." Looking around for any signs of sheep, I'm sure Peter felt like reminding his master that he, Peter, was a fisherman, his father was a fisherman, and his father was a fisherman. Tough fishermen do not chase stinky sheep around the fields (they catch stinky fish).

And then it all came back to him. One night all the disciples had been arguing about what position they would have when Jesus took over the Roman Empire. As they were debating among themselves, Jesus came over with a towel and a basin of water and began to wash their feet. It was as though He was saying, "Boys, do you really want to conquer the world? Do you really want to change things forever? Here's how it's done: wrap a towel around your waist, get a basin of water, and wash feet. We'll conquer the world when we learn to have a servant's heart."

Do you want to change your campus for the good? Do you want to change the attitudes of administrators, teachers, and fellow students? Would you like to see your campus become an effective missions force that would reach far beyond your institution's gates? Then do as Jesus did. Wrap a towel around your waist, get a basin of water, and become a servant to the people around you. We're called to minister not to nameless, faceless people, but to the people we live with, attend class with, eat with in the cafeteria.

It was a much older, much wiser Peter who wrote these words:

Feed the flock of God; care for it willingly, not grudgingly; not for what you will get out of it, but because you are eager to serve the Lord. Don't be tyrants, but lead them by your good example, and when the Head Shepherd comes, your reward will be a never-ending share in his glory and honor (*1 Peter 5:2-4, TLB*)

"JESUS THOWN EVERYTHING OFF BALANCE"

LIVING A LIFE OF SERVICE

JIM WILCOX

SERVICE IS THE WORD OF MY DISCIPLES. I served indeed, the humblest, the lowliest. I was at their command. My highest powers were at their service.

Be used. Be used by all, by the lowest, the smallest. How best you can serve? Let that be your daily seeking, not how best can you be served.

Truly man's thoughts are not God's thoughts, nor man's ways, God's ways. When you seek to follow Me in all, it frequently means a complete reversion of the way of the world you have hitherto followed. But it is a reversion that leads to boundless happiness and peace.

"Come unto Me all ye that are weary and heavy laden and I will give you rest."

Joy of the Weary I am; Music to the Heart I am; Health to the Sick, Wealth to the Poor, Food to the Hungry, Home to the Wanderer, Rapture to the Jaded, Love to the Lonely (Russell, *God Calling,* 30-31).

In her profound short story "A Good Man Is Hard to Find," Flannery O'Connor tells the tale of a three-generation family taking a traveling vacation in the family station wagon.

After making a wrong turn, they run into a small band of men they soon learn are running from the law, having committed a series of heinous crimes. The ringleader is appropriately called "The Misfit."

As he threatens to murder the grandma, she invokes the name and spirit of Jesus in order to bring peace to the horror surrounding her. She is trying to save her life. It is in The Misfit's response that O'Connor presents a theme that permeates most of her fiction: "Jesus thown everything off balance."

In other words, Jesus inverted life's purposes. Instead of seeking prestige and power as the world dictates, Jesus said, "Seek ye first the kingdom of God" (Matthew 6:33, KJV). Instead of making life a race to the front of the line, as the world teaches us, Jesus said, "The last shall be first, and the first last" (Matthew 20:16, KJV).

Instead of pursuing wealth and material comforts as our culture promotes, Jesus said, "Do not store up for yourselves treasures on earth. . . . But store up for yourselves treasures in heaven. . . . For where your treasure is, there your heart will be also" (Matthew 6:19-21).

Instead of seeking revenge when wronged, as our legal system encourages, Jesus said, "Love your enemies and pray for those who persecute you" (Matthew 5:44).

Indeed, Mr. Misfit, Jesus did "thow" everything off balance. He took away our microscopes and handed us telescopes. He overcame the temptation to be self-centered and gave himself for our salvation. He conquered the grave and provided us eternal life with Him in paradise. And the world has never since been balanced.

There are three principles to living a life of service, and to make them easy to remember, they rhyme. (I didn't study poetry and homiletics all those years for nothing!)

Attitude

When Mr. Brannich was much younger and fitter, he moved his little family into a new neighborhood where homes were bought and sold nearly as frequently as the Oklahoma wind blew.

For months, Mr. and Mrs. Brannich spent every evening and every weekend in their yard, planting sod, laying out flowerbeds, nurturing their new trees, and generally making their house a home. It took a lot of their cash, sweat, and hours, but within a couple of years their yard was as nice as any in the area.

About that same time, the house three lots down became vacant. The yard soon became overgrown with weeds. Incredibly quickly, that yard grew into an eyesore that sapped the vigor and energy from the entire neighborhood.

On his way home from church one evening, Mr. Brannich tried to ignore the lot as he drove past, but the Holy Spirit tapped his shoulder. *That's My house, Jack, and I need some help with it. Do you have a few minutes for Me?*

Mr. Brannich parked in his driveway, got his work clothes, gloves, and yard tools out of his garage, and headed east to "Jesus' house." Instead of working in his own yard in order to make it look great, Mr. Brannich now made this "dump" down the street his daily project.

"Jesus lives here and needs my help. How can I say no?" he told his wife, who began to help too.

After the yard was back to being presentable, the house was purchased by a wonderful Christian family who became the Brannich children's best friends.

In order to be like Christ, one must only treat each person with whom he or she comes in contact each day as if that person were Christ. That's Jesus stumbling out to His car with too many bags to carry. That's Jesus holding up that sign reading, "Will Work for Food." That's Jesus sitting alone in His prison cell.

No one who goes by the name "Christian" would turn a deaf ear or a blind eye to the Master in need. Right? It's called the attitude of *humility*.

Latitude

When one is liberated from the restraints of self-centeredness, looses the bindings of greed, and quiets the complaints of discontent, he or she will be free to serve others. With enthusiasm. With joy. With emancipation.

My students in Composition II are required every semester

to visit and report on a facility in the city that provides a service to the community: a homeless shelter, a church pantry, a counseling center, a rehabilitation center, or so on. The purpose is for each student to have an opportunity to study firsthand a social problem and one practical solution.

Through that assignment, many have turned their lives around 180 degrees. Some have changed their majors. Others have altered their semester schedules. Dozens have become volunteers at the facilities they visited—not for any self-gratification or glory but just for the fun of serving their Lord through serving their fellow human beings.

Several years ago my wife and I were having one of those months when the outgoing cash far exceeded the incoming checks. If it hadn't been for the two hams we got for Christmas bonuses from the school where we teach, we might have had little more than popcorn and rice to eat.

One day I was sitting in my office with the door closed when I heard someone sticking something on my door. "Oh, no—not another bill!" I cried from underneath my desk.

Mustering all the courage I could, I made my way to the door and found an envelope stuck to the other side. Inside were five $10 bills. My secretary revealed only that it was from a student, but she was bound to keeping it a secret. To this day, I don't know who God's angel was. It's called the latitude of *anonymity*.

Gratitude

Richard Carlson's book *Don't Sweat the Small Stuff, and It's All Small Stuff* (New York: Hyperion Publishers, 1997), has become one of my favorite books of all time. (And I don't even like nonfiction that much.)

In one chapter he writes,

Nothing helps us build our perspective more than developing compassion for others. Compassion involves the willingness to put yourself in someone else's shoes, to take the focus off yourself and to imagine what it's like to be in someone else's predicament, and simultaneously, to feel love for that person.

In trying to offer some assistance, we open our own hearts and greatly enhance our sense of gratitude. Compassion develops your sense of gratitude by taking your attention off all the little things that most of us have learned to take too seriously (17-18).

Carlson goes on to point out that compassion is both "intention and action"—the "Who needs me today?" intention and the "What am I going to do about it?" action.

My friend Stan Toler may be the most generous person I know. I used to have lunch with him fairly often when we served on the same church staff many board meetings ago, and few lunches went by without his picking up the tab for a table of students he knew or a family he had been counseling.

It became kind of a thrill for students to find out where Stan was having lunch and to show up and ask for a table in his view.

One day at a hamburger joint where Stan was eating, 30 students showed up. Without batting an eye, Stan asked for their tickets and paid them in full. It's called the gratitude of *generosity*.

"There is something magical that happens to the human spirit, a sense of calm that comes over you, when you cease needing all the attention directed toward yourself and instead allow others to have the glory" (Carlson, 25).

Part 4

LIFE SKILLS

The discovery of life lies on the daily and the ordinary, not the spectacular and the heroic. If we cannot find God in the routines of home and shop, then we will not find Him at all.

—Richard Foster

IS IT REALLY GOING TO BE WORTH IT?
UNDERSTANDING WHAT MY COLLEGE HAS TO OFFER
TYLER BLAKE

PHIL WASN'T SURE he wanted to be a "college boy." Lots of his high school buddies were already working and making pretty good money while he was stuck working part-time on the weekends and taking a bunch of classes on weekdays. At night he had to crack the books while they watched TV, played the latest video games, and partied. He found himself wondering, *Is college really going to be worth it?*

What do you think? It's definitely expensive, and it does take four of the best years of your life. Maybe you're thinking it would be better to find a job that will allow you to move up through the ranks. After all, in the four years it would take you to go through college, you could have been promoted four or five times, and . . .

OK—stop. College is, without question, worth it for most people. That's why 30- to 50-year-olds make up a large part of the market for colleges today. People who tried to take a short-cut and skip college are now coming to campus after 10 or 20 years in the workplace to earn their bachelor's degrees. Why? For some it's because they've hit a roadblock—they can't receive any more promotions without a degree. Others have simply matured enough to realize that college is a transformative experience, and they want that transformation. The following are just some of the benefits of getting a college education.

Money

Studies show that people with four-year college degrees

earn substantially more than workers with the same amount of experience but no degree. Even if money is low on your priority list, it can be demoralizing to know that your coworker who has half your experience is making twice as much money because he or she took the time to get a college degree.

Making big bucks is nothing to be ashamed of. John Wesley, the founder of the Methodist movement, said, "Gain all you can, save all you can, and give all you can." So if your goal is to be rich, make sure you recognize that any money or possessions that come into your hands are actually God's. He allows us to use things while we're here on earth to accomplish His eternal goals. When we finally stand before Him, we'll do so devoid of our German sports cars and Oakley sunglasses. We'll be penniless, naked, and in desperate need of His mercy, just like everyone else.

Career

True, lots of great careers don't require a degree, but what if, 10 years into a career, you decide you would like to look around? A bachelor's degree opens up a long list of careers that would otherwise be inaccessible to you. And even in jobs that don't require a college degree, like agriculture, fire fighting, or the military, most of the leaders do have degrees.

The great part about a degree is that it opens a world of possibilities. While college shouldn't be only a place for vocational training, it does fill that role. Whether your intended career is computers, farming, radio, television, or nursing, you'll find the college campus to be the best place to train yourself in the field of your choice.

Friends for Life

Now we're getting into the good stuff. You may have heard this before: "The friends you make in college are the friends you'll have for the rest of your life." This has been true for countless graduates for decades. Maybe it's because college comes at such a unique time and place. It happens during a time when you're just on the verge of being a mature adult. Most students enter college as teenagers and leave as adults. So in a sense, you "grow up" with your friends in college even more so than with your high school friends.

Likewise, college is a unique place where everyone is together with a common bond: to become better human beings. Who wouldn't want to be around people like that?

In college, assuming you live in college housing, you actually *live* with your friends. This is a huge difference from high school. Having a roommate is a terrific way to prepare for marriage and for getting along with people in general. Compromises must be arrived at on every issue from when lights will be turned out to who will get the top bunk. It's not all work, however. For most people, having a roommate is a blast. Roomies often become lifelong friends, because a bond forged on deep talks until three or four in the morning is hard to break.

Of course you'll make friends besides your roommate. In the dorm, students wander the halls freely, stopping in at open rooms just to say, "What's up?" Before you know it, you're heading out with a group of six or eight at midnight to dumpster dive! You'll also share meals with new people almost daily and meet interesting fellow students in your classes. By the end of your freshman year alone, your circle of friends and acquaintances will likely have expanded in ways you never imagined.

Spouse

Did I say we were getting to the fun stuff with friends? This is the fun stuff—dating! So fun that some people are accused of attending college for this reason only. In fact, many females have been charged with trying to acquire the elusive MRS degree. Get it?

While college isn't one big singles' club, it is an ideal place to meet that special someone. Why? Once again, because college is a place chock full of people who care enough to be the best they possibly can. Like the pioneers of the 19th century who sacrificed so much to travel west, college students give up four or five years and a significant bankroll all for the sake of bettering themselves. And with so many people like this around, the chances of meeting the one God has for you are that much greater.

Moreover, finding a spouse at college is easier for the same reason finding lifelong friends is. One recent study indicated that a month of college dating has the intensity of up to four months outside of college. This makes sense when you consider that you basically live at the same location, are able to eat every meal together, take classes together, study together —suffice it to say that there's the possibility for a lot of togetherness! For this reason, college students have to be extra guarded about how much time they spend alone and in what context. Still, if you want to get to know someone really well in a brief period of time, the best place to do so is on campus.

Time to Grow

More important than making friends or finding a spouse, college is a unique time to cement one's relationship with God. Christian colleges offer chapel services, prayer meetings, dorm Bible studies, in-class devotionals, and four years to chat with professors and fellow students about faith issues. Additionally, most secular universities also have places where Christian students can get together with others and grow together.

These opportunities coupled with newfound freedom allow many Christian young people to "own" their faith. Let me explain. As children we often follow the teachings of our parents and teachers without question. College can be a time when tough questions are asked, doubts are expressed, and possibly, crisis results. Yet if we persevere through such times, our faith finally becomes personalized as we "work out our own salvation." So this all-important four years of transition enables many to not only educate themselves about the Word but also internalize it and, most important, make it their own.

A Life

Remember when the old cut-down "Get a life" was popular? It was a phrase that basically meant, "You're a loser." College, for so many people, has provided a life: financial self-sufficiency, a satisfying vocation, trusted friends, a loving spouse, and a closer walk with God—in short, a life, a total package, much of which would not be there otherwise.

This is not to say that people who don't go to college don't have lives. The point here is that college is more than just a place where book knowledge is poured into one's head. It's a time of transition, hard work, soul-searching, and ultimately growing up.

And if you ask anyone who has ever completed four years, he or she will likely tell you—it's worth it.

ROOMMATES AND THE THEORY OF RELATIVITY
LIVING WITH A ROOMMATE
Kim Follis

DIGGING BACK THROUGH the annals of my college memories, I did a quick tally of my roommates. Lo and behold if I didn't share living space with four different guys and one girl —my wife whom I married the Christmas of my final year. If I learned one thing from my room-sharing experiences, it was the roommate theory of relativity.

This theory has to do with certain adjectives, most notably, "clean," "tasteful," "loud," "stinky," and "totally hilarious." Also involved are concepts like "ownership," "personal space," "foot odor," and "who paid last."

Allow me to illustrate. One roommate, who happened to be the goalie of the school hockey team (this was in Canada), thought that it was OK to store his gear in our room between practices and games. The point here is that one man's "pungent" is another man's "store that stuff in a snow bank!"

The roommate theory of relativity is rooted in our upbringing. You see, the parents whom we left either crying or smiling at the doorstep have actually come to college with us. I found this facet of the theory especially true in the case of my last roommate with whom I still live. All that self-differentiating you did as a teen was really all for naught. Deep in your subconscious, your parents ingrained the truth about important issues like whether or not it's OK to lick your fingers before sticking them back in the communal chip bag and the humor (or not) of redneck jokes. To paraphrase from the United States Constitution, "You hold these truths to be self-evident." Your mission for eight months is now not only to date the girl who sits in front of you in sociology class (see my last roommate) but also to enlighten your roommate of the truths that you hold dear.

The great irony is that your roommate is undertaking a similar mission. He or she, too, is controlled by the alien voices of his or her parents. Your roommate is seeking to save you from the error of your ways, lest you go through life offending others by the way you blow your nose.

Paranoid yet? Experiencing that prickly sensation of having your parents' voices speaking through you? Can you say, "the outer limits"? But since this is college, there must be a logical solution to the roommate relativity theory, and since this is a Christian college, Christian love should be a part of the equation.

The Roommate Theory of Relativity and the Stages of Community

The key to the roommate theory of relativity (RTR) is an understanding that living with a roommate is a journey that passes through several stages. I've adapted psychiatrist Scott Peck's stages of community to give us a bit of a framework. Jesus comes through with some sound advice on the subject. Got a roommate issue? Read on.

Stage 1: Pseudocommunity

This is the getting-to-know-you, everything-is-great stage of roommate life. During those first heady days of September, you're so happy to be away from home and at college that you're willing to overlook the borrowed belongings, the alarm that goes off 20 times every morning, the gargling, and the ketchup chips to name some more obvious possibilities. You give in and agree, avoid confrontation, invite the other person along when you're going out, and accept the other person's invitation even if bowling is not on your enjoyment list. You're the more mature person, and you're going to exercise maturity even if it means wearing a clothespin over your nose for the entire year. After all, your parents raised you to get along. If you managed to get along with your younger brother (who suddenly doesn't seem that bad), surely you can get past this set of idiosyncrasies.

Stage 2: Chaos

D-Day finally arrives. Someone drops his or her guard, eyes are rolled, a not-so-under-the-breath comment slips out, and an opening shot is fired and returned. You both reach into your parent-created store of expertise to debate what actually constitutes a pigsty. The flare-up is soon followed by avoidance, tension, forced smiles, and a secret petition to the resident adviser for a roommate switch. Here's the deal: Every relationship goes through chaos, including marriage (for you idealists). Here you discover the relativity of life. "Loud," "quiet," "clean," "messy," "obnoxious," "funny," "sappy," "sentimental," "tacky," and "cool" are really all relative terms. The way you perceive something may be the exact opposite of the way your roommate perceives the same thing. It's hard to recognize relativity when you're both so right.

Stage 3: Community

Finally, just as the cycle of flare-up and avoidance is about to repeat one more time and both of you are informed (secretly) by the resident adviser that your petitions for a roommate switch were shredded (along with all the others), someone, hopefully you, says, "Let's talk." So you talk. You use "I messages" and express your feelings. You actually listen to each other rather than wait for a chance to launch the next mortar bomb. To borrow a phrase from Stephen Covey, "You seek first to understand, then to be understood." Your own shortcomings come into view. You see the humor in your differences; you make some changes and agree to disagree on some things. You find a common relativity in the midst of your personal relativities and develop your own way of doing certain things.

It Takes Humility to Be a Roommate

Recognizing that your way of doing things is relative takes a large dose of humility. It's never easy to widen your view of anything. Notice how mad you get in class when the professor or another student challenges your carefully constructed view of the world? Humility opens our eyes and ears to other possibilities. Humility enables us to let go to the sometimes frightening possibility of being changed. Humility is scary, because it means letting go of the familiar and reaching for something new. Humility requires trust that the other person will respect you as you seek to travel a third way. Jesus, who had a few roommates of His own over His life, spelled out the need for roommate humility when He said (and I paraphrase),

> You can see the speck in your roommate's eye, but you don't notice the log in your own eye. How can you say, "Roommate, let me take the speck out your eye," when you don't see the log in your own eye? You're nothing but a showoff! First, take the log out of your own eye. Then you can see how to take the speck out of your roommate's eye (*Matthew 7:3-5, author's paraphrase of* CEV).

If your roommates do nothing more than help you get that log out of your eye, the experience will be more than worthwhile.

The Half-life of a Good Roommate

In his poem "Ulysses," Tennyson wrote, "I am part of all that I have met." In this poem, the aged warrior/adventurer realizes that all human touches shape our character and make us better people. This truth may be difficult to appreciate when your roommate's snoring awakens you at 4 A.M., but trust me—20 years from now it will come into focus.

I have the good fortune of living in the same city as all of my former college roommates. Even 20 years later, the bonds of friendship remain strong. I'm keenly aware of the contribution they made to my self-understanding and the texture of my life. In our time of greatest need we reach out for those people who know us best and will accept us in spite of our circumstances.

In a dark time in his life another warrior/adventurer, Paul, wrote a letter to Timothy with whom he roomed on the road. He says to his friend, "Do your best to come to me quickly. . . . Do your best to get here before winter" (2 Timothy 4:9, 21). If we're willing to do the hard, humble work of getting through the psuedocommunity and chaos of roommate relativity, we can develop a few of those rock-solid relationships of the Paul/Timothy variety that stand the test of time.

THE REDEMPTIVE RHYTHM OF LIFE
HOW TO BEST MANAGE YOUR TIME
Dean Blevins

AT FIRST GLANCE, college looks pretty organized. College living has a basic rhythm shaped by class times, semester breaks, holidays, and final exams. You would think life would be simple.

Think again. When you start piling up the "extras," your schedule can become pretty complicated: assignments, friends, assignments, work, assignments, service projects, assignments, dating, assignments—and ultimately exams. Negotiating the demands of college life takes organization.

Most time management strategies work well in organizing our day and semester:

- We begin by first charting (usually in 30-minute blocks) how we currently use time. This way we spot "gaps" and wasted time during the day.
- We also place all our class assignments and other schedules on a central calendar, and we develop a plan for meeting each major assignment based upon the smaller, simpler tasks that must be accomplished along the way.
- Then we begin to prioritize the tasks we have and schedule specific times each week and throughout the semester to meet our goals. The more we can meet the smaller tasks on time, the better chance the major assignment will be well done.

These steps can be done fairly simply with a little planning. The process really helps us survive our scheduling problems, if not the unscheduled crises we face. We get things done, we feel confident in our ability to manage our lives. We survive classes and actually do well in many of them.

But is this all that time management accomplishes? Once we get the strategies down, is there something more that we're supposed to do with our time? Is not the purpose of time management not only to accomplish our goals but also to master time?

Controlling time seems to be the emphasis of our culture these days. The previous generation talked of labor-saving devices. Today, with cell phones, E-mail, fast food, and interactive video, we seem to live in a time-compressed world. Our day disappears as we negotiate the myriad distractions we face. Often the more time we have, the more we feel we need to do. Do we manage time, or does time manage us?

God seems to offer a different form of time management that is both creative and redemptive. The first five books of the Bible reveal a creative rhythm to life. The first chapter of Genesis tells us that there are times of creative activity and times of Sabbath rest. There is an order to the basics of life that God has established. From Exodus through Deuteronomy, God makes it clear to the nation of Israel that there are also times for work, times to care for each other, and times for worship (Exodus 23:12-20; Leviticus 23; Numbers 29). In the midst of God's shaping a nation called Israel, the people were commanded to order their lives into a rhythm dictated by God. Through the biblical story we learn that God commands us not only to be creative but also to include times of rest and worship so God can re-create within us passion and capability.

God is the master of time the same way He is in charge of all aspects of life. God understands that people need to order their lives but that they also need to live in sync with the goodness of His creation. In a sense, we're stewards of creation. Jesus uses this concept in His parables to describe the terms "faithful" (Luke 12:35-38, 42) and "unfaithful" (Luke 16:1-8; 19:12-27; Matthew 25:14-30) stewards. The apostles also use it in describing Christians (1 Corinthians 4:1-2; Titus 1:7; 1 Peter 4:10). A steward is one who has more responsibility than a servant but nevertheless does not possess what he or she manages. This includes how we spend our time. In actuality, we're called to practice time stewardship rather than time management. Rather than allowing time to control us, we faithfully utilize our time to honor God.

God has also given us creative opportunities. We're often told that we're the masters of our lives, but this is not so. We are born helpless into the world and survive through the care of others: either from parents and loving relatives or from strangers working in maternity wards we never know. We grow up in environments that nurture and challenge us to various degrees: families, schools, clubs, churches, and organizations that prepare us for this opportunity. God has provided the means to get us to where we are today. Now we're asked to become stewards of the very care others have given to us to this point. The church has understood time as a pattern as well, beginning with its early history. In most congregations we celebrate a kind of "rhythm" to the church year. We celebrate times of birth, times of achievement, times of sending, and times of homecoming. We acknowledge that God is deeply involved in the basic course of our lives through practices like baby dedications, baptisms, Sunday School promotions, retreats, camps, graduation banquets, homecomings, marriages, retirement celebrations, and even funerals.

In addition, God has also given us some stewardship in how we *redemptively* use time to live our lives. Time has a redemptive rhythm that many congregations observe yearly. They celebrate meaningful moments that prepare for and commemorate the birth of Jesus through Christmas and the four weeks leading up to Christmas, called Advent. Churches often use special Sundays and particular weeks of the year to remember the purpose of Jesus' ministry on earth (starting on January 6 with Epiphany) and our call to discipleship through a period of the year called Lent. This season begins on Ash Wednesday around 45 days before Holy Week, a time given to remembering Jesus' last days in Jerusalem. We also take time to remember Jesus' ultimate gift through His death and resurrection (the Easter season) and the birth of the Church through the power of the Holy Spirit (Pentecost). Each year, following this rhythm, we're asked to order our lives around God's redemptive "time management." We live a part of each year intentionally celebrating and remembering what the Gospels teach about who Jesus is and what He has done for us.

Even each week is marked by special times. We gather regularly to worship, to learn about God, and to serve others and the world. Each day we're asked to find time for prayer, reading scripture, and living our Christian walk. God has graciously provided for us our redemption and asks us to be stewards of our time so we can grow into a deeper Christian life. We do not save ourselves, but we're given stewardship of God's saving grace in our lives. We're given the means by which we can both remember and respond to what God has done for us through yearly, weekly, and daily practice. Such timely living not only strengthens us for the challenges we face but also matures us into deeper Christlikeness.

Time stewardship is crucial in any setting. Many persons have found themselves shipwrecked because they did not follow God's order of creative and redemptive time. God gives us the ability to be wise and faithful stewards in His kingdom if we'll respond.

Stewardship includes taking care of ourselves creatively and redemptively. It means taking advantage of the opportunities God has graciously given us at this point of our lives. In basic practices of day-to-day life, we're encouraged to care for our bodies through sleep, proper eating, exercise, and basic hygiene. We're also asked to care for the mental, emotional, and interpersonal aspect of our lives by relating with people, reading, and thinking, taking time to reflect seriously on who we are and how we feel. We order our lives to Jesus' redemptive story, we worship, and we practice our faith daily. Our lives are organized by who we're called to "be" in God's eyes. Who we become is crucial since God has given us stewardship of our personal lives.

Time stewardship is important in an academic setting.

Take the time management practices suggested at the beginning and use them according to God's purpose. Take time at the beginning of each semester to wisely schedule times for study; for rest and recreation; for worship, devotion, and fellowship. Plan out major assignments so they're manageable and completed over the time given. Be aware when extra time will be needed to prepare for exams and finish your papers. You may have to adjust the schedule as you go, so take the time to review where you are each week.

Frankly, God has given us this timely opportunity in our lives to attend college. Many students have found themselves shipwrecked because they did not manage time carefully in fulfilling academic responsibilities. More than survival, we need to be intentional in planning our learning so that we get the most out of the opportunity. If we do this, we'll enjoy a rich legacy of learning. God has given you this opportunity. Therefore, be a wise steward.

IT'S NOT A MATTER OF "IF"—IT'S A MATTER OF "WHEN"
LEARNING HOW TO STUDY

Jim Wilcox

"I BELIEVE IN BEING FULLY PRESENT," Morrie said. "That means you should be with the person you're with. When I'm talking to you now, Mitch, I try to keep focused only on what is going on between us. I am not thinking about something we said last week. I am not thinking of what's coming up this Friday. I am not thinking about doing another Koppel show, or about what medications I'm taking.

"I am talking to you. I am thinking about you."

I remembered how he used to teach this idea in the Group Process class back at Brandeis [University]. I had scoffed back then, thinking this was hardly a lesson plan for a university course. Learning how to pay attention? How important could that be? I now know it is more important than almost everything they taught us in college (Mitch Albom, *Tuesdays with Morrie* [New York: Doubleday Publishers, 1997], 135-36).

Learning how to pay attention is at the heart of learning how to study in a university setting. Believe your professors and parents when they tell you that if there's ever going to be a place and a time in life when you are inundated with diversions and distractions, it will be while you're in college. And if you can't learn how to focus and concentrate amid this constant din of activity, you're in for a long four years. Or six. Or seven.

Learning how to study—how to pay attention—is really learning how to be a responsible adult. And whether you learn it now, in the academic setting of a college classroom, or later, in the vocational setting of an office building, you *will* learn it.

Unfortunately, the longer you wait to accept and adopt this principle of successful living, the higher the price you'll end up paying. Learning to be responsible is one of the earliest and most powerful signs of personal integrity, and any mentor you listen to will advise that your integrity is the beginning of your success. Without it, you're doomed to a lifetime of failure.

Everyone has to find his or her best style of learning. Each classroom on your campus this semester will probably have at least one representative of the following student-types, so keep your eyes peeled.

Bart Joiner has never met an organization he didn't love. He's been president of the marching band, vice president of the chess club, secretary of the Spanish club, fry cook at the local McDonald's, volunteer at the nursing home, and tenor in the church choir. And that was just last year.

Jack Pratt is just the opposite. Jack doesn't do squat. The only thing you can really count on with Jack is not being able to count on him at all.

Jack's best friend is Hardy Party, the campus clown. His social calendar is so jammed up that he couldn't squeeze study time into it if you lent him a giant grease gun. His motto is "Party On, Dude."

Hardy sure admires the cutie who sits next to him in chapel—Paula Perfect. She's got it all—perfect body, perfect hair, perfect eyes, perfect teeth. She has a 4.0 grade point average, a full-ride scholarship, a brand-new Jetta convertible, and a photographic mind. She's smarter than most of her teachers.

But Paula hates Bertha Brownnoser, the biggest kiss-up this side of Jay Leno. She bats her formidable fake eyelashes at the teacher as if she's fanning the king of Siam, pretending to hang on every word that she's pretending to scribble down with the speed of a court reporter.

Her roommate is Melody Mediocrity, the student with the constant smile embedded across her blank face. For her, a 500-word assignment is just wasting paper.

Melody has found the perfect match in her boyfriend, Peter Procrastinator. This guy missed his high school graduation because he was stuck in study hall making up all his final exams.

Chances are you know most if not all of these students (and I use that term loosely). You may even have gotten a little uncomfortable at the familiarity of some of these descriptions.

My friend and fellow writer Jim Priest has published a book titled *Family Talk,* in which he provides a fine set of steps each of us should follow in order to become more productive and disciplined individuals. I've borrowed his points and elaborated on them here.

1. Recognize yourself for what you are.

You're a human being who has trained to put off a task until you think it just might go away all by itself. Unfortunately, the pressure your procrastination puts on you makes an otherwise simple chore almost overwhelming. The good news is that you can change your behavior and learn to become a person who acknowledges and accepts deadlines.

2. Begin with small things.

You can set daily goals at which you can succeed, setting the tone for bigger objectives and bigger successes. Commit to yourself (even write it down) that for three consecutive nights you will be in bed by midnight. Or commit that for a week you will have tomorrow's homework finished *and printed off your computer* before you go to bed.

3. Just keep going.

Perseverance and maturity go hand-in-hand. Everybody slips and falls. It's called "the agony of defeat." But defeat is as fleeting as the task at hand, and the successful student learns his or her lesson from a failure and prepares doubly hard for the next challenge.

4. Surround yourself with people who are also trying to be disciplined.

If the adage "Misery loves company" is true, then so is the idea that "we really do need each other." One Alaskan husky, no matter how strong and determined, cannot pull an Arctic sled more than a few inches by itself. It takes a dozen or more, working in concert, to get the sled across the icy tundra.

5. Don't forget the reward.

This does not refer to the rewards you can't control, such as specific grades or job offers. This refers to those you *can* control: the weekend trip home after acing a midterm exam, a night out with the people or person you love after completing a big research project, or a good night's sleep.

The surest way of learning how to be disciplined is to *schedule in your study time.* Actually write it down in your planning book, and always plan on more time than you honestly think you'll need, because interruptions will invariably come. Murphy's Law is so true: "If something *can* go wrong, it *will* go wrong."

The next step is to *develop a set of rituals.* The reason we get excited about Christmas is that the tree in the front window and the lights around the roofline signal that the season is drawing near. We know the holiday is right around the proverbial corner, because we hear the carols and smell the eggnog.

This is a great process to follow in order to create the atmosphere to study. Maybe you'll want to study with a certain type of instrumental music on your stereo. If so, then reserve that particular CD for study time so that every time you hear it, you know it's time to crack open the textbook.

Some people like to wear a certain outfit. Others develop a tradition of turning off the phone, the pager, and the television. Some shower first. Others have to lock the doors and close the curtains. Find your own set of study "customs" or habits that will "put you in the mood," and stick to them.

One of the most important habits to have is to *gather all your materials and supplies* so that you won't have to jump up and down, searching everywhere for that book or page or pen or whatever. If you have everything you need at hand, you'll spend your time actually studying instead of merely preparing to study.

If you're like me, you can't work without a snack nearby, so be sure to raid the appropriate machines ahead of time. And if this looks like it could stretch into an all-nighter, colas and coffee are great sources of caffeine.

Just like selling real estate, the three secrets to successful studying are *location, location, location.* Let me tell you from experience—studying in bed is just asking for trouble, as is trying to study with your girlfriend or boyfriend. The dorm can be too noisy until about 2 A.M., so that may be out. Even going to the library is a social event for far too many students.

Interestingly, some locations are great places to study at *certain times.* Afternoons or early evenings are actually the quietest times of the day in the dorm and library, so as much as possible, try using those times to study.

The final secret is to *attack the attack plan.* Follow through with your commitment to get your schoolwork finished on time. Don't put it off until the last minute. Most professors don't accept late work, so break that bad habit today.

Learn to be disciplined. Learn to be independent. Learn to be a responsible adult. Count on it—you're going to have to learn it sooner or later, and life is far easier when you learn it sooner.

TOOLS OF THE GIFTED

PRACTICING GOOD STEWARDSHIP

Elliot Johnson

We have different gifts, according to the grace given us (*Romans 12:6*).

OFTEN A ROOKIE IS PROMOTED to the major leagues and billed as a "five-tool" player. Such a label means the athlete is a star in the making, for he can hit, run, field, throw, and hit with power. Many have gone on to excel and become legends. Willie Mays, Hank Aaron, Dave Winfield, Ken Griffey Jr., Alex Rodrieguez, and Derek Jeter are examples. Others have never realized their potential and have lost opportunities because of alcohol, drugs, or poor work habits.

God has given all of us varying amounts of time, talent, money, opportunities, and physical and mental abilities. Some of us are "five-tool" players. Others of us have fewer tools with which to work. But we can excel in the time and place where God puts us and "star" on His team. With God's grace, we'll refine our assets, prepare diligently, and recognize the opportunities He gives us.

We're not our own. Our bodies belong to God, who formed us from the dust of the earth and then redeemed us. First Corinthians 6:19-20 says, "Do you not know that your body is a temple of the Holy Spirit, who is in you, whom you have received from God? You are not your own; you were bought at a price. Therefore honor God with your body." Since we do not own the physical body, we can strive to keep ourselves in good physical condition for our Master's use. Among other things, this means that regular physical exercise is part of the spiritual worship due our Creator (Romans 12:1). It means we must be alert in our eating habits, both in quantity and quality of food. We must avoid the sin of drunkenness. If we never take a drink of alcohol or use illegal drugs, we will never fall prey to those addictions. God's plan is also for us to avoid sexual contact with anyone to whom we're not married.

Our money and our possessions are on loan to us from God, and we are stewards. Certainly, giving to God and His cause is important. But God is even more concerned about how we spend what we keep. Do your spending habits reveal a value system based on eternal perspectives? The parable of the talents demonstrates that our eternal rewards depend upon how we use the material possessions God has given us (Matthew 25:14-30).

Mickey Mantle was a gifted baseball player. He hit 536 home runs, was a part of seven World Series Championship teams with the New York Yankees, and won three Most Valuable Player awards. Some people believe he could have been the greatest player who ever lived. But Mickey partied as hard as he played. Alcohol diminished his skills, caused his body to grow old prematurely, and dulled his mind. It sabotaged the greatest combination of speed and power in baseball. Mickey's gifts were trashed by his excesses, and he was kept from reaching even greater physical heights. As he neared death in 1995, he made a heartfelt plea for others to avoid the mistakes he had made. "Don't be like me," he humbly declared. "I'm no role model." Regretting his selfish lifestyle, Mickey asked Jesus to save his soul and received the forgiveness he so desperately needed. Mickey went to heaven only by the grace of God, the only way any of us will make it.

Just as all of us have some physical gifts, all Christians have one or more spiritual gifts. Romans 12:6-8 says, "We have different gifts, according to the grace given us. If a man's gift is prophesying, let him use it in proportion to his faith. If it is serving, let him serve; if it is teaching, let him teach; if it is encouraging, let him encourage; if it is contributing to the needs of others, let him give generously; if it is leadership, let him govern diligently; if it is showing mercy, let him do it cheerfully." God will both use us and reward us for the faithful use of our gifts. One of His ways of guiding our lives is to show us our strengths and encourage their development. Often He uses other people to show us. Pastors, teachers, and parents can be a big help. He gives us gifts for a purpose and would not expect our gifts to be unused. Do you know your spiritual gifts? Are you using them faithfully? Do you continually seek opportunities to use them further?

Eternal rewards are based upon how we've used the tools God has given us. They're based upon the faithful use of those we have, not upon those we don't have. Many people have been given more resources (tools) than they realize. An ancient Persian legend tells of a wealthy man by the name of Al Haffed who owned a large farm. One evening a visitor told him of fabulous amounts of diamonds that could be found in other parts of the world and of the great riches they could bring. The vision of all this wealth made him feel poor by comparison. So instead of caring for his own prosperous farm, he sold it and set out to find these treasures. But the search proved to be fruitless. Finally, penniless and in despair, he committed suicide by jumping into the sea.

Meanwhile, the man who had purchased Al Haffed's farm noticed one day the glint of an unusual stone in a shallow stream on the property. He reached into the water, and to his amazement he pulled out a huge diamond. Later, when working in his garden, he uncovered many more valuable gems. Poor Al Haffed had spent his life traveling to distant lands seeking precious jewels, while on the farm he had left behind could be found all the precious stones his heart desired.

Are you using all the time, talent, and treasure God has given you for His glory? You may have more resources than you realize! When you use what you are given as He provides the opportunities, you'll find fulfillment and success!

TO WORK OR NOT TO WORK

LEARNING TO BALANCE SCHOOL AND WORK

TYLER BLAKE

ONE EVENING, sitting down to a dinner of steaming pork chops and apple sauce, Jennifer, a high school junior, asked her parents if they thought she should work when she went off to college.

Jennifer's mom said, "Absolutely no work while you're in college. School comes first. You can work in the summer only. I'm not helping pay your tuition just to have you bring home C's and D's on your report card."

But her dad said, "Just because you're in college doesn't mean you can't work fulltime. That's what I did. Yes, sir—I went to school during the day and swept up at the tire factory at night. Those were tough times, all right, but that's what made me the man I am today!"

"What were your grades like?" asked Jennifer's mom.

"Well," her dad replied, "They weren't too bad. I had a C average. But back then a C was a C. No one made a B just for showing up and an A for handing something in! You had to get your grades the old fashioned way—you had to earn them."

"That's what I thought," said her mom. "A C average."

Jennifer was perplexed. Should she plan on working or not? She decided to do some research and continue the conversation some other time. During the next few weeks, she checked out books and periodicals at the library and spoke with several admissions counselors on the topic. She discovered that most students work to help defray expenses, but nearly all struggle to balance work and school. She did, however, locate the following helpful guidelines.

1. Working during college depends mostly on your schedule and financial need. If you plan to engage in a lot of extracurricular activities like band, choir, or student government, finding time to work will not be easy. And if you intend to play a varsity sport at your college, work may not be an option at all, at least during the season. Many coaches don't allow their players to work, and even if they did, there wouldn't be much time for it given the demands of practice and conditioning on top of class and homework.

The key word is *need.* If your parents are paying your tuition, thank the Lord and work less, study more. If they're also paying your room and board, thank the Lord vehemently, hug them every day, and work only in the summer (but save your money carefully during this time).

2. Don't work full-time. Although some students do work full-time and go to school full-time, it's not a good idea for several reasons. For one, you won't have much time to study, and this could well affect your grades. It may also be more difficult for you to schedule the classes you need and have the energy to attend these classes regularly, on time, and with a high degree of alertness. And since your college record stays with you for the rest of your life, you should care about your grade point average.

Also, you won't have time to make friends or attend lots of school functions like basketball games, concerts, study groups, devotionals, and informal get-togethers. This may not seem important to you now, but when you're 45 years old, you may wish you had gotten to know more people and used your college years for going to class, studying, and making friends.

3. See yourself as a college student until you graduate. Commit yourself to being a "college kid" until you get your degree. Embrace this role; don't be ashamed of it. Wear your college sweatshirt with pride! In the 1920s, being a college student was the coolest thing you could be—it was "the age of the undergraduate." And college students changed the world in the 1960s. So don't let your friends from high school who chose not to continue their education make you feel bad about this.

And don't listen to relatives or anyone else who tells you that you should be supporting yourself and holding down a job instead of wasting time at school. Go to all the activities you can. Run for student office. Work for the yearbook or newspaper. Play intramural sports. Do whatever you can to be involved and meet others. It may be hard at first, but you'll look back fondly on these times and pat yourself on the back for being bold enough to get out there and mix with others.

4. *Don't neglect your part-time job.* Even though school takes precedence, don't blow off your part-time job. Do your best at it while you're there, but forget about it when you're not. Make sure your employer understands that you are first and foremost a college student and that this job is a temporary way to help fund you. But keep in mind that, even while you're creating a college transcript of grades and hours, you're also compiling an employment record that will follow you through life. When you finally graduate from college and are ready to begin your career, your part-time employers will be contacted to find out about your work habits. Were you on time? Did you work hard and show initiative? Begin now making your name as a dependable, hardworking employee.

5. *Don't work at a job that consumes all of your time, attention, and energy.* Beware of jobs that try to "own" you while you're in college. Shy away from so-called "management" positions promising a salary with full benefits. These jobs are often a smoke screen for greedy employers who want you to work 60-70 hours per week for 30-40 hours of pay. Don't take a job where you're "on call," and avoid jobs promising easy money selling knives or vacuum cleaners unless you're thick skinned enough to tolerate people treating you rudely and telling you no frequently. Plus you have to be disciplined enough to make your own schedule and stick to it religiously.

Consider a physical job that will allow you to exercise and give your mind a rest. There are lots of part-time jobs that allow you to move around and release pent-up energy from hours of class work and study. Parcel delivery services give you the opportunity to work up a sweat, make good money, and forget about school for a while. (You *won't have time* to think about school!) Custodial positions involve inside work that mostly involves emptying trashcans and vacuuming in big office buildings. If you like the outdoors, lawn services are always looking for new people. Finally, there's no shame in flipping burgers, and waiting tables can be a fun job that brings in a lot of instant cash.

6. *Beware of the debt monster!* Many college graduates walk away with a diploma—and an enormous debt. Loans for college are very easy to acquire, but remember: they're easier to get than they are to get rid of. College students are borrowing more than ever. And the reason for this debt, surprisingly, is not rising tuition costs but that students spend more of their money on nonessentials, like clothes, cars, and computers, and less is leftover for tuition. Therefore, great discipline is required of the college student. During these four years, take pride in driving an '85 Toyota wagon or any other "clunker." Hey—you're a college student! This is your one chance to live below your means. Buy your clothes at The Salvation Army store. Eat at the student union or cook instant noodles in your room. The more frugal you are during these years, the happier you'll be with yourself when you graduate. And pay no attention to your high school friends who are "living large" because they chose not to go to college. In four years you'll leapfrog them in both earnings and knowledge.

Having acquired this vast cache of knowledge, Jennifer brought up to her parents a few weeks later the subject of working while in college. This time she presented them with several worthwhile facts and statistics. Together they decided that a part-time job, working around 20 hours a week, would be perfect for Jennifer's financial situation. She also decided to work full-time in the summer and begin saving now for tuition, books, and room and board. *After all,* she thought, *it's never too early to get ready for college.*

WHAT'S YOUR IQ?
DEVELOPING A LIFESTYLE
OF INTEGRITY
Jan Lanham

AS A STUDENT, you've become familiar with all kinds of evaluations, and you know that IQ (intelligence quotient) scores serve as one indicator of a person's range of potential. There's another kind of IQ that speaks to a different side of your development—your integrity quotient. Limitations in this area of life can hinder anyone.

All you have to do is pick up a newspaper or listen to a news broadcast to know that our society is questioning the integrity of people in just about every arena of life. From government leaders to those in business, law enforcement, journalism, medicine, research, academic institutions, and even faith communities, the actions of too many have left us disappointed and confused. Society has sought to reduce the arena of integrity to ever narrowing domains. "Don't judge my private actions." "Don't hold me accountable." "It's everyone else's fault." What do we really mean when we speak of integrity?

We often think of truth-telling as a function of integrity, and we've seen that virtue in pitiful short supply in our society. Yet integrity is more than that. Perhaps at its most basic level, to speak of integrity is to speak of wholeness, continuity, and cohesion as one integral unit. To be sure, we're complex persons who perform many different roles, and we may not always be able to present the same face in all situations. Yet through the many varied aspects of our personalities, our roles, and our relationships, we need to strive toward a healthy sense of congruence and authenticity if our lives are to be characterized by integrity.

Congruence alone is not enough. Hitler's outer actions of

destruction were congruent with his inner experience of hatred. A life of integrity must also speak to the content of the inner and outer life.

As we live as Christians, allowing God to work with us and through us, our actions need to cohere with our words; our inner and outer lives need to be cut from the same fabric. Yet these must also cohere with the words of Christ. What are the values and commitments that form the core of our being? Do our actions consistently reflect those values? When we're made aware of those times when a disconnection occurs, can we be courageous enough to be accountable for our actions? As Christians, do our chosen values, expressed and lived out, accurately reflect our relationship with Christ?

An interesting exchange is recorded in the 23rd chapter of the Gospel of Matthew, in which Jesus confronts the Pharisees and the teachers of the Law. These were good people who were trying to live out the tenets of the Law to demonstrate their righteousness and integrity as Jewish leaders. Yet Jesus points out that they had missed the larger truths. They had become consumed with specific prohibitions in their religious culture but had missed out on the larger, life-affirming principles that Jesus heralded in His kingdom.

In this discussion, Jesus gives us a glimpse of the values of His new order and helps us to understand some of the qualities that characterize a life of integrity. "But do not do what they do, for they do not practice what they preach . . . on the outside you appear to people as righteous but on the inside you are full of hypocrisy and wickedness" (Matthew 23:3, 28). Jesus quickly identifies the need for consistency, authenticity, and congruence. He was not impressed by outward appearances but looked to the inner motivations and desires of the heart. He was not content to stop with congruence but went on to discuss the values that motivated actions and the compelling themes that molded decisions.

Jesus first laid the groundwork by presenting a vision of right relationships. He cared about how people treated each other. In verse 4, Jesus painted an interesting image of the

Pharisees: "They tie up heavy loads and put them on men's shoulders, but they themselves are not willing to lift a finger to move them." A life of integrity takes relationships seriously. Are our relationships grounded in respect, love, mutuality, and reciprocity? Are we willing to balance our needs with those of others? The Pharisees had sought to take care of their own needs at the expense of others. There was an unhealthy sense of entitlement in the actions of the Pharisees; they carried the expectation that they were above others. Jesus sought to level the playing field and to recognize the value and needs of all around him—children, women, men, outcasts, rich, and poor.

In contrast to the Pharisees' desire to be seen by others, honored and recognized for who they were, Jesus puts forth the values of humility, equality, and servanthood as operating principles of His Kingdom. All are to be honored, as all are to recognize the need to serve one another. A life of integrity acknowledges that each person has value as a child of God. We can put this into action as we seek to serve rather than to be served.

A life of integrity acknowledges the need to confront the issue of priorities. Jesus recognized that while the Pharisees had kept the letter of the Law in relationship to the tithe, they had missed more important concerns. "You give a tenth of your spices—mint, dill and cummin. But you have neglected the more important matters of the law—justice, mercy and faithfulness" (Matthew 23:23). The Pharisees were admirable in sharing out of their goods, but they stopped at the strict fulfillment of the requirements. Jesus again points us to a more expansive, far-reaching vision for the concerns that should characterize us. Justice, mercy, and faithfulness! How different our world would be if the inner passions of our lives for justice, mercy, and faithfulness found their way into outer actions toward our neighbors!

One way to think of justice is doing the right thing: to be honest and fair in our relationships with others, to be accountable to others for our actions, to actively seek to bring about right relationships in our world by addressing issues of injustice, oppression, prejudice, and hatred. To do these things is to concern ourselves with the issues that Jesus also faced in the society around Him. A life of integrity acknowledges that we're connected to others and that what happens to others is indeed our concern.

To drink deeply in the waters of mercy that God has opened before us is to seek also to be merciful to those we encounter. Jesus spoke often of those who willingly received the gifts of grace and mercy but who failed to respond to others with similar gifts. A life of integrity is grounded in the awareness that God's gifts of mercy and grace are not to be hoarded but are to be returned with a grateful heart in service to others.

To experience God's faithful embrace and His steadfast love for us is also to accept the call to reach out to others in faithful love and concern. The story of God's faithfulness is imprinted throughout human history, and God's presence will accompany us on our journey as well.

While it's easy to find fault with the Pharisees in their pursuit of righteousness and integrity, we cannot ignore that the call to live out the values and commitments expressed by Jesus comes to us as well. Perhaps if Jesus were to talk about the 21st century, He might point out those occasions when we have treated some graciously and ignored others, when we have pursued career aims by stepping on the backs of others, and when we have judged people by what they own rather than by who they are. Perhaps He would remind us of those times when we did not tame our words and thus destroyed reputations, when we have turned a blind eye to those in need around us, and when we have treated our financial or academic commitments carelessly. Or would He remind us of how we have ostracized instead of included and where we have criticized rather than encouraged?

The call is just as clear and compelling for us today. A life of integrity comes from the commitment of our whole lives to the Lordship of Christ and the willingness to both hear and live out His teachings in authentic and congruent ways. Are you willing to commit your life to the Lordship of Christ? Are you willing to live out His teachings? In other words, are you willing to live a life of integrity?

CONCLUSION

JIM HAMPTON

It has been many years since I graduated from college. Yet I still remember my time there as if it was yesterday. The time I spent studying, playing, meeting new people, encountering God, and preparing for my lifework has made me the person I am today. Each event and relationship I had the privilege to participate in had a profound influence on my life.

While attending a college reunion a couple of years ago, several friends and I gathered to eat. Although it had been years since some of us had seen each other, it took only minutes before we felt as if we had never really been apart. We began recounting stories of one another's exploits and adventures while in college, and we laughed deeply into the night. As we were reminiscing about our college days, we were all reminded of the powerful influence that attending college had on each one of us. We had come from very diverse backgrounds and were now involved in diverse occupations. Yet we had a common bond due to the experiences we shared together, the life we lived together, and the God we sought to live for—together. Today my college friends are scattered all over the world. Yet we still have that bond that ties us together—our college experience.

At this point in your life, graduation may seem like a long way off. Attending a college reunion probably doesn't even seem to be a remote possibility—you've got to get through your chemistry midterm first! So why do I offer these words to you? For this reason—I want you to recognize now the incredible impact that your college or university will have on you if you allow yourself to experience all that it has to offer. Be intentional about the way you approach your interactions with the people you encounter, the classes you attend, the ministry you involve yourself in, and the memories you make. Being intentional about these things now will ensure that when that glorious day of graduation finally arrives, you'll be able to recognize the indelible mark that this experience has placed on your life.

As we close, please accept this blessing (adapted from Numbers 6:24-26) from all of us:

> *May the LORD bless you in your studies and keep you in right relationship with Him as you enter into this new life experience called college; may the LORD make His face shine upon you and be gracious to you as in turn you extend grace to others; and may the LORD turn His face toward you and give you peace when you are wondering what in the world you have gotten yourself into.*